PRAISE FOR THE BOOK OF JOB

"A richly thought-provoking, and passionately thoughtful, interpretative encounter with a crux biblical text that has baffled humanity down through the ages and that here receives a truly worthy response."

— Thomas L. Pangle, Joe R. Long Endowed Chair in Democratic Studies, University of Texas at Austin

"Irving M. Zeitlin's The Book of Job is a brilliant philosophical and ethical analysis of that canonical work – and of much of the scholarly attention devoted to it – that supports his conclusion that Job – the book – is a theological scandal. Zeitlin's critique of the Jobian scholarship (and of the Jobian God) is impeccable and his argument in support of Job is cogent. Zeitlin's style in presenting this simple but profound philosophical education makes it a delight to read."

— Donald Wiebe, Professor of Divinity, Trinity College, University of Toronto

"In this learned engagement, the distinguished sociologist, Irving Zeitlin, offers a meticulous exegesis of the Book of Job and a critical colloquy with a host of prominent scholars who have sought to plumb the mysteries of this disturbing composition. Central to Zeitlin's analysis is a theology/theodicy contrast between the amoral, "beyond good and evil" Cosmic deity depicted in Job, and the ethical, Covenantal God of the Torah and the Prophets."

— Joseph M. Bryant, Professor of Sociology & Religious Studies, University of Toronto

The BOOK *of* JOB

A THEOLOGICAL SCANDAL

IRVING M. ZEITLIN

Copyright © 2017 Irving M. Zeitlin. All rights reserved.

No part of this book may be used or reproduced in any manner whatsoever without written permission of the publisher.

ISBN: 978-1-936961-337

Books are available for special promotions and premiums.

For details, contact: specialmarkets@linxcorp.com.

Book design by Paul Fitzgerald

Published by LINX

LINX, Corp.
Box 613
Great Falls, VA 22066
www.linxcorp.com
Printed in the United States of America

Cover Artwork by Esther Zeitlin
"Job Afflicted"

TABLE *of* CONTENTS

Part One – The Jobian Text: 1
   Regarding the "Patience of Job" 9
   The Absence of the Covenant 11
   The Deity's Response to Job 14

Part Two – A Dialogue with the Commentators: 19
   The word Satan in the Hebrew Bible 23
   Was the Original Jobian Text Modified? 33
   The Book of Job: Its Idiosyncrasies 45
   The Book of Job: A Failure 52
   Additional Profound and Challenging Commentaries .. 62
   "God is Dead?" 85
   Epilogue – Covenantal Duties: A Credo 91

Endnotes 95

Works Consulted 97

About Irving Zeitlin 99

PART ONE
THE JOBIAN TEXT

In strong and unambiguous terms, the opening sentence of the Book characterizes Job as innocent, upright, God-fearing and as a man who turned aside from evil. The Almighty himself attests to that fact, stating, "That there is none like him on the earth" (1:8). Job was not only righteous and pious; he was also, as it happens, extraordinarily prosperous. Indeed, he was "the greatest of all the children of the East."

As a righteous man and loving father, Job was not only concerned that he himself should do what is right, and express a love and fear of God in his heart; he was equally concerned, in that regard for his children, his seven sons and three daughters. So when the sons invited their sisters to their customary feasts, Job, fearing that the sons might have sinned in their hearts, offered burnt-offerings on their behalf (1:5). Let us therefore note, that Job expected punishment for sin, whether overt or in one's heart. This observation becomes relevant later, when we consider the claim some scholars make, that a central question of the Book is whether there exists any such thing as an exquisite, *disinterested* love of God.

Job knew not, nor would he ever learn that he has become

the subject of a heavenly discourse in God's court, where the so-called "sons of God" (*benei Elohim*), including *HaSātān* ("the Satan"), have presented themselves before the Lord. *HaSātān*, who has just returned from a sojourn on earth, is addressed by the Lord who, calling attention to Job, states that there is none like him on earth where innocence and righteousness are concerned. This provides *HaSātān*, meaning literally "the adversary," with the opportunity he has been waiting for. Whose adversary? Primarily Job's, of course. But is there not a sense in which he is also God's adversary in this bizarre drama? Although the full evidence supporting a resounding "yes!" to that question must await a later stage of our analysis, it will suffice, for the present, to underscore the fact that *HaSātān* possesses enough autonomy to persuade the Lord to "test" Job. The point of the "test" – the afflictions to which Job will soon be subjected – is to ascertain whether there is a direct link, as *HaSātān* has alleged, between Job's piety and his prosperity; whether if God, through the agency of *HaSātān*, were to put forth His hand and touch all that Job possesses, he would blaspheme God to His face. God thus agrees to place Job in *HaSātān's* power, the sole proviso being, that he must not kill him.

So Job's ordeal begins: his oxen and asses are taken in a raid and the attending servants are slain; a fire from heaven consumes Job's sheep and their shepherds while bands of Chaldeans slay still other servants and steal their camels. Worst of all, Job receives word that while all of his children were dining in their eldest brother's house, a great wind struck the house, causing it to collapse, killing all of them.

As one reads the text relating this chain of events, one is shocked and dismayed: Is this the ethical Deity of the Hebrew Bible whom the Jobian author presumes to describe here? Did not the author recognize the outrageousness of attributing to the God of justice the slaying of all those innocents – animals and humans alike? The sheep were, after all, innocent victims of the "test," as were the servants; and the biggest outrage of all, the taking of Job's children. Imagine the cynicism which the author ascribes to the Lord (*Yahweh*), that in killing Job's children, Job was not being afflicted personally; that afflicting Job's flesh, would constitute for him greater suffering than losing all of his beloved children. And what about Job's wife, the mother of those deliberately destroyed children? How did the author of the Book imagine that the Lord would countenance such deeds, causing an innocent woman and mother to suffer such a calamity for the sake of His "wager" with *HaSātān*?

One must wonder how the Jobian author could have presumed to ascribe to God a willingness to become an accomplice to such a scheme. Nowhere else in the Hebrew Bible does a narrative posit a celestial being capable of inciting God to participate in unjust and evil acts. And yet, in Chapter Two of the Jobian text, when once again *HaSātān* has returned from earth, and God calls attention to Job's holding fast his integrity, the author has God acknowledge not only His own complicity in the atrocities perpetrated against Job, but also His less-than-omnipotent status before *HaSātān*:

> Thou didst move Me against him, to destroy him without cause. (2:3)

Moreover, the author unashamedly portrays the Deity as agreeing to continue the experiment, permitting *HaSātān* to attack Job's bone and flesh, but short of taking his life. *HaSātān* thereupon smites Job from head to foot with boils so terrible that to relieve himself somewhat from the pain and itch, he sits among the ashes scraping his flesh with a potsherd. When Job's wife – whose name we never learn and who is treated by the author as a nameless, non-person – observes Job in his agony and urges him to "bless" (i.e., to curse) God and die, he reprimands her for her base talk and continues to refrain from sinning with his lips. This, however, is only the beginning of Job's ordeal, for there is much more in this anomalous text that strikes one as theologically scandalous.

Enter Job's friends, who have heard of Job's tragedy and have come, apparently, to commiserate. Hence, in Chapters Three through Six, we see that in the presence of Eliphaz, Bildad and Zophar, Job curses the day he was born, wishing the doors of his mother's womb had never opened, and that he had died in her womb or perished at birth. Eliphaz subscribes to the dominant doctrine of retribution of the time, that great suffering is a consequence of great sinning. Eliphaz addresses Job as one whose habit it has always been to instruct others, but now who has fallen among the great sufferers. Eliphaz proceeds to espouse the prevalent doctrine that the innocent and upright do not suffer, and that it is only those who sow mischief and plow iniquity who provoke God's anger. Eliphaz therefore counsels Job to turn to God and plead his case before Him; for the Lord is just, Eliphaz avers; He saves the weak and needy from the hands of the strong, and redeems from troubles and war. Job, for his own good, should therefore remember the Lord's justice. But Job responds that if his calamity were weighed in the balance, it would be heavier than the sands of the East. Oh, he cries, if God would only grant the things he longs for to be crushed and cut off, *though he is innocent of any wrongdoing, and has never denied the words of the Holy One.*

Temporarily accepting Eliphaz's assumption that God rewards the righteous and punishes the wicked, Job pleads with the Lord to instruct him so that he may understand wherein he has erred. He beseeches the Lord to look upon him, for surely he would not lie to the Lord's face. Thus pleading that the Lord return to him, Job courageously protests that his cause is just. Enter Bildad the Shuhite, who also subscribes to the dominant doctrine, that great suffering betokens great sinning. Like Eliphaz, Bildad has come, ostensibly, to comfort Job but upon hearing his protestations of innocence, confronts him with the doctrine. But now, in Chapter Nine, Job begins to challenge the dominant doctrine, that suffering implies sinning, that suffering, as a consequence of sinning, is divine punishment for it.

As we reflect carefully on the content of Chapter Nine, we the readers know with certainty that Job is neither sanctimonious nor undeservedly claiming his innocence, for the Deity Himself has attested to Job's piety and righteousness. To understand Job as he understands himself, therefore, we need to view him as an individual who has critically examined his conduct and conscience, and has found no good reason for his torment. Hence, Job's undeserved suffering strengthens his resolve, even in his agony, or especially because of it, to struggle for justice – to prove to the Almighty that He has wronged an innocent man. But Job asks himself, how can a man struggle with God? How can a mere human contend with the Almighty, Job asks, as he recounts God's marvels and powers. Job understands that his struggle is a matter of seeking justice. But how shall he gain the opportunity to argue his case? It now begins to occur to Job, that the dominant doctrine of retribution may be false. Is it possible, he muses, that the Almighty destroys the innocent together with the wicked, and even mocks at the calamities of the guiltless? Does He give the earth into the hands of the wicked? And if it is not the Lord, who, then, is responsible for this state of affairs?

Job's utterances now openly challenge the dominant doctrine as he strives to make his case. As there is no arbiter or umpire who can decide between Job and God, Job raises his voice so to speak: If God would only take His rod away and cease to terrorize him, he would speak his mind without fear. He would gain the courage to demand of God an explanation of why He destroys this poor being whom He has made of clay, and whom He has resolved to bring into dust again.

How right Job was to ask, "If it be not He, who then is it?" For it is certain, as we know, that it was none other than this amoral, Jobian Deity who handed Job over to the tormentor and murderer. What we have here in Job is a great-souled individual who knows, as we do, that he has committed no offences so great as to deserve the catastrophe that has been visited upon him, and the afflictions he continues to suffer. The horrors to which he is subjected have made him weary of life; and yet, weary though he is, he will grow bolder in stating his grievance before God.

Enter Zophar, in Chapter 11, who accuses Job of having uttered a "multitude of words," of being full of talk and boasting that he is pure and clean not only in his own eyes, but in God's eyes as well. Job is blind to his own iniquity, Zophar asserts, and the Lord has exacted from him less than his iniquity deserves. Zophar then introduces a new motif, which has been enthusiastically embraced by several distinguished commentators – the motif of God the "mysterious," whose ways are unfathomable. For Zophar, there are certain deep things and purposes of the Almighty that are simply beyond human comprehension. Job, however, is becoming more resolute in rejecting the doctrines espoused by Zophar, Bildad and Eliphaz, his so-called friends and comforters, who are no comforters. Now Job himself recounts the marvels of God to demonstrate to his friends that what they know about God's powers, he knows as well as they.

For Job, however, God's powers are beside the point. For as we see in Chapter 13, Job knows and has always known God's powers quite well. The Almighty's *powers* were never in question. What Job demands and desperately needs is God's justice. Job's friends are not only false comforters; they are "plasterers of lies" who do him a grave injustice by implying that his tragedy is *prima facie* evidence of grave transgressions. Job therefore becomes unrelenting in his determination to achieve justice for himself before God – a determination in which Job's strength of character and nobility shine through. Bolder than earlier, Job speaks his mind, come what may.

Why, he asks, has the Lord singled him out for such torment – a torment especially painful in light of the *this-worldly* character of the Hebrew Bible. Job knows that if ever he is to be justified, it must be while he still clings to life, there being no afterlife, no other world in which he can be vindicated. As if, therefore, to impress the Deity with the seriousness of his plight, and the urgency of his plea – indeed his *demand* for a fair hearing before the Almighty, Job reminds Him of the brevity of human life.

In Chapter 15 as earlier, Eliphaz accuses Job of arrogantly displaying neither fear of God nor devotion to Him. Why, he asks, does Job allow himself to get carried away, turning his spirit against the Lord and uttering words that can do no good? Rebuking Job for claiming a wisdom and understanding that his friends do not possess, Eliphaz describes himself as among the "gray-headed" and "very aged" men, which suggests that Job was younger than the three friends who have become his detractors. For Eliphaz, greater age means greater wisdom. For him, therefore, there can be no explanation for Job's torment other than his putative transgressions.

Job, however, remains undaunted. How long, he asks in Chapter 19, will his comforters who are no comforters, continue to vex his spirit and cause him additional anguish with their excoriating words? Have they no shame to deal so harshly with him, striving to magnify themselves at his expense? Job has somehow intuited the truth, that it is none other than the

Lord who has visited the calamity upon him, and it is the Lord who owes him a hearing. Hence, what Job demands from his friends is not merely compassion, but acknowledgement of the possibility that the hand of God has touched him, though he is innocent. He wants them to grasp the truth as he does, that even as he is being destroyed, he will, at the last, be vindicated by God Himself.

Indomitably, Job therefore continues to call for an explanation from the Almighty, cautioning his friends at the same time not to rush to false judgment in his regard. It is as if Job is admonishing them: Look about you, for heaven's sake! *Do you fail to see that the wicked everywhere are triumphant and joyful, while the just and innocent languish as I do?* But Job's admonition falls on deaf ears.

As Zophar proceeds with his attempted repudiation of Job's grasp of his situation, the accusations he levels at Job are groundless. For although Zophar speaks in general terms about the destiny of the wicked, his words appear to be directed against Job personally. He accuses Job of oppressing and forsaking the poor and needy, which we know is untrue. Zophar, like his friends, is drawing unjustifiable inferences from the prevalent but mistaken doctrine, that great suffering indicates great sinning. Job rejects the doctrine not merely from his own experience, but from his open-eyed observations of the human condition. *Indeed, what is most outrageous of all, says Job in Chapter 21, is that while the wicked enjoy the fruits of their evil ways, they openly exhibit insolence toward God.* Like Zophar earlier, Eliphaz in Chapter 22 continues to accuse Job personally of having engaged in "oppression" and "exploitation," again a totally groundless accusation, that is actually an inference from the false notion of a direct causal link between suffering and sinning.

Regarding the "Patience of Job"

If Job is "patient," it is in a sense quite different from that which has been accepted from the time of James' epistle (5:11), if not earlier. Let us note that in Chapter 21:4 Job asks, "Why should I not be impatient?" [*Madua lo tiqzar ruhy?*] So if Job is "patient," it is only in the sense of being adamant and unrelenting in his demand for a direct and personal dialogue with the Almighty, to persuade Him that he, Job, is entirely blameless.

In one's very first reading of the Book of Job, one confidently looks forward to an encounter between Job and the Almighty in which He shall finally feel obliged by His *covenant* to answer for the unspeakable crimes perpetrated against Job and his loved ones, with the Lord Himself as accomplice. Surely, the Deity will ultimately heed Job's plea for justice. But, of course, it is under the taken-for-granted assumption that Job is engaged with the one and same ethical and covenantal Deity of the rest of the Hebrew Bible, that Job "patiently" but resolutely continues to demand and await the opportunity to be tried and thus to "come forth as gold."

When, in response to Job, in Chapter 25, Bildad the Shuhite speaks again, he fails to address Job's point. Instead, he celebrates God's powers, not his justice, reducing humanity to a mere worm or maggot. In Job's reply in Chapter 26, though he cannot but acknowledge the Almighty's boundless powers, he nevertheless asks how Bildad's celebration of God's powers speaks to Job's grievance. In Chapter 27, though God's powers are not relevant to Job's ordeal, he joins in the exaltation of the Almighty and even appears to reaffirm the presumed validity of the doctrine of retribution in spite of his earlier repudiation of it; the apparent reason being to warn his detractor-friends, that given *their* belief in the doctrine, they had better exercise caution: for if they continue unjustifiably to condemn him, they are liable to share the destiny of the wicked.

In the continuation of Job's parable in Chapter 28, he recounts some of the remarkable accomplishments of human beings, ostensibly to drive home a fundamental moral point that is relevant to all other times as well. Ah, yes, Job is saying, impressive achievements indeed. But, for all their so-called accomplishments, human beings have failed to recognize that which is of greatest moment: "Behold, the fear of God, that is wisdom; and to depart from evil is understanding" (28:28). So we come to Job's profound point: obedience to the Almighty's ethical commandments, and a fear of all the terrible consequences if the commandments are disobeyed. Indeed, it is said, in effect, in Chapter 29, that Job practiced what he preached, delivering the poor who cried, and the fatherless who had none to help them.

In Chapter 32, we see that the three men have ceased to answer Job because of the insistence on his innocence. Elihu even becomes angry, his wrath kindled against Job because he continues to justify himself. Elihu could not, of course, have known that when he spoke of the possible role of an angel as intercessor, Job not only had none in the heavenly court, but had, instead, a deadly adversary. Far from defending Job as Elihu had claimed was his original intention, he effectively joins the other detractors in scorning Job for his having come to imply that God Himself has, *for some unknown reason*, turned against him. This proves to Elihu in Chapter 34, that Job has definitely joined the company of the workers of iniquity.

The Absence of the Covenant

Elihu's utterances in 35:1-8 are not only antithetical to the covenantal theology of the Hebrew Bible, it anticipates the bizarre conception of the Deity in Chapter 38, where the Almighty finally condescends to speak to Job out of the whirlwind. Taken literally, Elihu's words assert that the Almighty cares not at all whether human beings are righteous or not; wickedness and righteousness are solely human concerns, not God's. The absence from the Book of Job of the quintessential concept of Covenant thus makes the Book problematic in the extreme. Indeed, in addition to all the other idiosyncrasies to which we have called attention, it needs to be recognized that the absence of a covenantal relationship between the Deity and humans must be regarded as a fundamental theological defect.

In the Covenant with the Israelites of Exodus 19:5, described again in Deuteronomy 7:6, it is said that if they will hearken to God's voice, they will be His own "peculiar" treasure from among all peoples. Moses' explanation of God's choice is essential for an adequate understanding of the passage. Why did He set His love upon the Israelites? As Moses stated, not because they were especially numerous, nor because they were especially virtuous -- Moses attributed no such qualities to them. The reason for God's choice lies in the conception of Him as an *ethical* Deity who heard the cries of an oppressed people and came to their aid because He despised oppression. It was an act of grace, but a conditional one: if they will obey His commandments and thereby keep His Covenant, then they will become a "peculiar treasure" to Him. The meaning of "peculiar" in this context is clear: all nations of the world are God's by reason of His power, but the Jews are His not only by reason of His power, but also and *especially by reason of their own consent and Covenant.* The italicized passage is the animating principle of the entire Hebrew Bible, and of the historical self-understanding of the Jewish people.

In the Book of Job, there is no mention at all of Israelites, which in and of itself has no special significance, since that is also true of other books of the Bible. And as there is no mention of Israel, one would not expect the Jobian author to have integrated the Israelite Covenant, either explicitly or implicitly, into his narrative.

But long before God made that Covenant with a specific people, and long before He made one with Abraham, He made an explicit Covenant with Noah in which all nations and individuals of the world would be judged on the basis of *ethical principles and commandments*, and rewarded and punished accordingly.

According to the Rabbinical tradition, long before the revelation at Sinai there already were laws binding on all human beings. The laws were called "Noahide," because from Noah's sons "the whole world branched out (Genesis 9:19). The Rabbis established six such basic laws: (1) humans may not worship idols; (2) they may not blaspheme God; (3) they must establish courts of justice; (4) they may not murder; (5) they may not commit adultery; and (6) they may not rob. A seventh law was added after the flood: (7) humans may not eat flesh cut from a living animal. The command to Adam (i.e., all humans) in Gen. 2:16 was taken to mean that all humans have a concept of God and are therefore forbidden to blaspheme Him or worship idols. Alas, one hears not the faintest echo of these principles in the words and actions of the Jobian Deity. Worse, while Job violated none of these commandments, the Deity violated the most important commandment of all: He became complicit in the murder of innocents.

As we listen to Elihu in Chapter 36, we again hear him defending the same doctrine that the other friends have espoused all along. At the same time, however, Elihu advances another conception of the Deity, in which the very essence of God is a *mystery*, a notion we shall challenge in due course. Elihu is intent upon celebrating the omnipotence of God, attributing to Him all the workings and phenomena of nature – thunder, lightning and other awesome, natural spectacles. Addressing Job personally, the burden of Elihu's remarks is the greatness of God's *powers*, and the corresponding puniness of human beings. Elihu's speech thus sets the stage, as it were, for the Almighty's boasting in Chapter 38f.

The Deity's Response to Job

We come now in Chapter 38 to the dramatic climax of the Book. As one reads the concluding chapters carefully, pondering the implications of the speech which the author of the Book has placed in the mouth of the Deity, one is stunned. For the speech totally ignores Job's just grievances, while the Deity declares that the cosmos He has created is an amoral realm, in which the petty concerns of the human condition are of no real interest to Him.

Poor Job! All he has asked for from the very beginning of his ordeal is a hearing, never for a moment doubting the Deity's mightiness. Yet, in Chapters 39 and 40, in response to Job's plight, the Deity simply flaunts His powers in a crescendo of sheer braggadocio, reminding Job of His mastery over "*behemoth*" and "*leviathan*". Some scholars have interpreted these creatures as symbols of primordial cosmic forces with which Yahweh had once contended and over which He prevailed in order to establish His dominion. Other scholars have noted, however, that the text describes "*behemoth*" as a quite earthly creature, a herbivore that eats grass as does an ox; and "*leviathan*," too, as an earthly sea-creature, however large, fierce and formidable it might have been. Such scholars have, therefore, identified "*behemoth*" with the hippopotamus and "*leviathan*" with the crocodile (or whale). The problem with this view is obvious – that we would hardly be impressed to read that the Deity, who is described as "Almighty," had once gained mastery over such creatures. Hence, the view of the former scholars who propose that the Jobian author employed "*behemoth*" and "*leviathan*" as symbols of cosmic forces, appears to be more plausible. But that view, too, would be problematic in the extreme, as we shall see.

In polytheism, gods do contend with one another and with natural and cosmic forces. In the Hebrew Bible, however – bracketing the Book of Job for the moment – we can see that in accordance with the monotheistic intuition, there are no such forces which Yahweh had to overcome in order to establish His rule of the universe. One might wish to challenge this assertion by asking, "What about the numerous allusions in the prophetic books and in the Psalms to the revolt of the sea and the rivers in the primordial era of the world's history, and to their subjection to Yahweh?"

We may reply to this question by considering the following: nowhere in the Hebrew Bible, neither in the primeval legends of Genesis 1-11, nor in the prophetic and poetic literature, is there the faintest suggestion of a *cosmic* force, principle, or condition that Yahweh had to overcome in order to establish His supremacy. What we find instead, are certain ideas that originally had emerged in polytheistic cultures, but which subsequently were radically transformed; no longer natural or cosmic forces, they became *historical* and *ethical* concepts.

In the Ugaritic poem, for instance, where Baal contends with *Yam*, the sea-monster, we read:

> Lo, thine enemies, O Baal, lo,
> Thou shalt smite through, lo
> Thou shall exterminate thy foes.

If this is compared with a like passage in the Psalms, we readily discern the significant differences between them. In Psalm 92:10, we read:

> For, lo, thine enemies, O Lord,
> For lo, thine enemies shall perish:
> All the workers of iniquity shall be scattered.

Here the enemies of the Lord are identified as evildoers; and the evil in question is social and moral. Similarly, we read in Psalm 89:10:

> Thou rulest the proud swelling of the sea;
> When the waves thereof rise, Thou stillest them.
> Thou didst crush Rahab, as one that is slain …
> Righteousness and justice are the foundation
>   of Thy throne;
> Mercy and truth go before thee.

And in Isaiah 27:1, the prophet says:

> In that day the Lord with His sore and great and strong sword, will punish leviathan the slant serpent, and leviathan the tortuous serpent; and He will slay the dragon that is in the sea.

Here, as in the Psalms, it is clear that the prophet employs "leviathan" as a symbol of human sin and evil. This is evident not only from the entire context, but also from the immediately preceding paragraph where he says:

> For, behold, the Lord cometh forth out of His place to visit upon the inhabitants of the earth their iniquity. (Isa. 26:21)

The same interpretation applies to the mention of Rahab in Psalms 74:12-14; 87:4; and 89:10. What originally was a mythological monster, a dragon, is applied in the biblical literature to Egypt. The myth is historicized and employed metaphorically to describe Yahweh's extraordinary victories in history, most notably over the Pharaoh's forces at the time of the Exodus (Isa. 30:7; 51:9).[1]

How, then, in that light, should we interpret the employment of the terms "behemoth" and "leviathan" (and Rahab, 9:13; 26:12) in the Book of Job? Certainly, it would be a ludicrous trivialization of the Almighty's power and majesty to suggest that the intended reference is to earthly beasts such as the hippopotamus and the crocodile, though the passages in question do appear as such a trivialization. On the other hand, given the amoral nature of the Jobian Deity, who shows no concern for humans and justice, one can hardly claim that "behemoth" and "leviathan" are metaphors for Yahweh's great victories over human evil in history. Hence, those who propose that in the Book of Job these beasts stand for cosmic forces appear to be more convincing. What that means, however, as has already been suggested, is that in this respect as in all others to which we have called attention, the Book is an anomaly in the context of the Hebrew Bible.

When we read Chapter 41 – whatever might be the significance of those earthly creatures – one thing is undeniable: nowhere in the Deity's speech is there a single word of attention to Job's condition, plea and grievance. Furthermore, as one reads the final Chapter (42), one cannot help noticing a total change of character in Job. The stalwart rebel who until this moment has stood up to the Deity, suddenly becomes contrite. Overwhelmed and overawed, apparently, by the Deity's *power*, Job is portrayed as acknowledging his insignificance and settling for that, instead of justice. The courageous and rebellious Job was, evidently, unacceptable to the redactors who, therefore, made him penitent.

We are told in the concluding chapter – an Epilogue of sorts – that the Lord changed Job's fortune and gave him twice as much as he had before, including new children, seven sons and three daughters – as if this could ever compensate him and "Mrs. Job" for the originally unjustifiable loss of their beloved children. But even this cynical and transparently contrived epilogue acknowledges – perhaps inadvertently – that the Deity of this bizarre tale had in fact perpetrated evil against an innocent and just man, and against his innocent loved ones – not to mention all the other innocent victims of the Deity's wager with *HaSātān*. For we read in the end, that Job's brothers, sisters and acquaintances came to show Job sympathy and to comfort him "*for all the evil that the Lord had brought upon him*" (42:11, italics added).

PART TWO
A DIALOGUE WITH THE COMMENTATORS

In their critical and exegetical commentary on the Book of Job[2], S.R. Driver and G.B. Gray propose that although the Jobian author's distinctive outlook on life, as revealed in his work, is never directly stated or formulated, one can characterize that outlook in the following terms: that God did not send sufferings on humanity merely for the reasons commonly assigned, and that it is not necessarily true that as an individual suffered, so he had sinned. The Author had presumably discovered

> not only that God did not abandon the sufferer, but also that suffering and loss had not detached him from God, that it was possible to serve and love God not for the outward things He gave, but also for what He was in Himself.(li)

One must ask, however, how the authors can assert that the Jobian Deity did not abandon Job the sufferer, after having taken from him his beloved children, though they were innocent of any offense against Him. One wonders, moreover, why one would love the Deity of Job "for what He is in Himself" – a

Deity with which humans cannot form any real connection, an amoral Deity who ostensibly cares not at all about humanity or justice in the human condition.

For Driver and Gray, it is "the Satan's" role to dispute the inherent worth of Job's character. Job, he insinuates, had served God not for God's sake, but in order to obtain the handsome price of such service:

> human nature is incapable of pure devotion to God, human conduct is not *disinterested*; if the payment for it ceases, or becomes uncertain, man's service to God will cease, man will no longer address God reverentially, or affectionately, but blasphemingly; where love and trust had seemed to be while such qualities received their price, their hate and contempt will certainly be when the price is withdrawn. Such is the issue between Yahweh and the Satan, Yahweh upholding, the Satan calling in question, the integrity, the sincerity, the *disinterestedness* of Job. (lii, italics added)

So one must ask not only how it is possible to love the Jobian Deity for Himself, but also what would prompt one to offer Him a "disinterested" love.

Following Driver and Gray, other outstanding commentators have proposed that "disinterestedness" is a central issue or motif of the book, so we shall need, in due course, to address these questions: Is "disinterestedness" really a central concern of the book? Does Job exhibit a truly "disinterested" devotion to God? Does Yahweh's speech out of the whirlwind (or His "wager" with the Satan) suggest anywhere that He demands such a love from humanity? Is a totally disinterested love of God humanly possible? Does the covenantal God of the Hebrew Bible demand a disinterested love? Indeed, does the New Testament demand such a love? Does Yahweh's speech and therefore the author offer us a positive theory of the meaning and purpose, if any, of suffering? And does the author somehow connect the theory with a call for a disinterested love of God?

Driver and Gray suggest that Yahweh's speech

> accompanies an appearance of direct manifestation of Yahweh to Job, and in this respect is the direct response of Yahweh to Job's deepest desire: Job has at last found Yahweh; and, in spite of the rebuke of his words beyond knowledge, he has found Yahweh on his side, no more estranged from him than in the days of his former prosperity, but more intimately known; as compared with his former, his present knowledge is as sight to hearing, as direct, firsthand personal to secondhand and traditional knowledge. So far from his earlier sense of God's friendship having been shown by his sufferings to be a delusion, its reality has been vindicated, and by God's response to his appeal his communion with God has been intensified. (lx-lxi)

But this interpretation is problematic in the extreme. Where in Yahweh's speech is there anything that warrants the claim that "God's friendship" has been shown and its reality vindicated? It certainly was not Job's deepest desire to gain mere "communion with God"; what he desired and demanded was a hearing and a vindication before God. The Deity's speech, however, at no point acknowledges the injustice of the catastrophe suffered by Job and his wife, and all the other innocents who perished as a consequence of the Jobian author's peculiar conception of the Deity.

Driver and Gray are inclined to class the text with the wisdom literature. They recognize, however, that the text differs in at least two respects: in its combination of prose and poetry, the prologue and epilogue being prose, the speeches poetry; and in its use of dialogue. Not too long before Driver and Gray published the first edition of their commentary in 1921, Horace M. Kallen's *The Book of Job as Greek Tragedy* appeared. In that work Kallen proposed that the author of the Book of Job was a Jew profoundly influenced by Euripides, which accounts for the general form of the book, and for the use of dialogue in particular. In rejecting Kallen's thesis, Driver and Gray argue that the Book of Job is no more similar to a Greek or any other epic or drama than to other works of Hebrew literature (xxii-xxiii, fn.#5). In their brief but convincing rebuttal of Kallen's thesis they cite the critical review of Kallen's book by C.G. Montefiore who proposed that the Job poem

> culminates in a god to whom prayer is useless and idle, and who, in His truest nature, is essentially beyond and indifferent to what man calls good and evil.[3]

Montefiore was among the first if not the first to employ the Nietzschean phrase "beyond good and evil" to describe the Deity of the Book of Job. Since that time, several other distinguished commentators have either used the same phrase or have described the Deity in what amounts to the same terms.

So the issues we need to explore could not be clearer: who needs a God who is beyond good and evil? Or as any intelligent child might ask: what is such a God good for? And what does the Book of Job's message, as expressed in the Deity's speech, imply for personal religion?

If we now proceed to examine some of the outstanding commentaries on the Job text, with special attention to these issues, we need to begin with the fundamental question concerning the Jobian Deity's relationship with *HaSātān* and the implications of that relationship.

The Word Satan in the Hebrew Bible

The Hebrew word *Satan* means "adversary." In 1 Samuel 29:4 the word is used by the Philistine princes as they observe David and his men, who have fled from Saul, gathering in their rear as if to join them in battle against Saul's forces in the Valley of Jezreel. The princes ask Achish their king, "What do these Hebrews here?" rightly suspecting that David is employing a stratagem and has no intention of actually allying himself with the Philistines against Israel. Achish tries to persuade the princes that David is loyal, but they respond angrily:

> Make the man return, that he may go back to the place where thou hast appointed him, and let him not go down with us to battle, lest in the battle he become an *adversary* to us; for wherewith should this fellow reconcile himself with his lord [i.e., Saul]? Should it not be with the heads of these men? Is not this David, of whom they sang one to another in dances, saying: "Saul hath slain his thousands, and David his ten thousands?"

Achish is thereupon compelled to send David and his men back to Philistia.

In 2 Samuel 19:22, Shimei the son of Gera, who earlier had cursed David, hastens to Jordan so that he may fall down before the King and beg his pardon. David is ready to forgive him, but Abishai the son of Zeruiah intervenes, saying that Shimei should be put to death because he had cursed the Lord's anointed. David, however, replies:

> What have I to do with you, ye sons of Zeruiah, that ye should this day be as an *adversary* unto me? Shall there any man be put to death this day in

Israel? For do not I know that I am this day King over Israel? And the King said unto Shimei: "Thou shalt not die."

In 1 Kings 5:18, Solomon, having been anointed King, sends a message to Hiram of Tyre informing him that whereas Solomon's father, David, could not build a temple for the Lord, owing to the wars he had had to fight, the Lord has given Solomon peace on every side:

> There is neither *adversary*, nor evil occurrence. And, behold, I propose to build a house for the name of the Lord my God, as the Lord spoke unto David my father saying: Thy son, whom I will set upon thy throne in thy room, he shall build the house for My name.

In Kings 11:14,23,25, we are told that Solomon had numerous foreign wives and that he had built shrines for them where they offered sacrifices to their gods. Solomon, it is said, thus did that which was evil in the sight of the Lord. To punish Solomon, therefore, the Lord raised up an *adversary* unto Solomon, Hadad the Edomite (11:14).

> And God raised up another *adversary* unto him, Rezon the son of Eliada, who had fled from his lord Hadadezer King of Zobah. And he gathered men unto him, and became captain over a troop, when David slew them [of Zobah]; and they went to Damascus, and dwelt therein, and reigned in Damascus. And he was an *adversary* to Israel all the days of Solomon, beside the mischief that Hadad did; and he abhorred Israel, and reigned over Aram. (11:23, 25)

In the Book of Numbers 22:22, 32, the word occurs in the legend of Balaam, sent by the Moabite King to curse the children of Israel who had recently come out of Egypt. Although the Lord refused to permit Balaam to carry out his mission, he nevertheless rose up in the morning, saddled his ass, and accompanied the princes of Moab:

> And God's anger was kindled because he went; and the angel of the Lord placed himself in the way for an *adversary* against him. (Num.22:22)

The word occurs again a few lines later when Balaam's ass, frightened by the sight of the angel, lies down under Balaam who angrily beats the animal with his staff. But then Balaam also sees the angel who says:

> Wherefore hast thou smitten thine ass these three times? Behold, I am come forth for an *adversary*, because thy way is contrary unto me; and the ass saw me, and turned aside before me these three times; unless she had turned aside from me, surely now I had even slain thee, and saved her alive. (22:32)

The original sense of the word Satan as "adversary," is still found in Jesus' employment of the word in his reprimand of Peter in Matthew 16:23, where Peter, upon hearing Jesus say he must go to Jerusalem to suffer many things and be killed, rebukes him, saying: "God forbid, Lord! This shall never happen to you." Whereupon Jesus turns to him and replies: "Get behind me, Satan! You are a hindrance [or stumbling block] to me ..."

In addition to this original, simple meaning of *satan* as "adversary," "hindrance," or "stumbling block," it is found in the Hebrew Bible only four times either as a title or as what has been regarded, perhaps mistakenly, as a proper name: in the

Book of Job 1:6,12, and 2:1, with the definite article *ha*, e.g., *HaSātān*; in Zechariah 3:1, again with the definite article; and in I Chronicles 21:1 as what some scholars have interpreted as a proper name. In these passages, Satan appears as a distinct being, as in Chapter One and Two of the Book of Job where he is one of the "sons of God," bearing the title, "the Satan." He is a member of the celestial council of angelic beings who have access to God's presence. In the Book of Job, the Satan is Job's adversary, as we have seen, who falsely accuses him before the Almighty of being a potential sinner. In this role *HaSātān* is definitely invested with a malevolent character. In most of the traditional commentaries on the Book of Job and on the role of *HaSātān*, it is observed that he has no power to act without divine permission, and that he cannot, therefore, be regarded as the embodiment of a power that opposes the Deity. As we have seen, however, *HaSātān* in the Book of Job is in fact endowed with considerable autonomy, enough to enable him to play the despicable role of inciting or *causing* the Lord to afflict Job.

In the Book of Zechariah, *HaSātān* ("the Satan") again plays an accusatory and adversarial role, but without the far-reaching consequences one finds so repugnant in the Jobian drama. Zechariah prophesied in the time of Darius, when the Judeans were in exile under the domination of the Persian empire. In the prophet's vision he hears an angel ask the Lord how long will He not have compassion on Jerusalem and the cities of Judah,

> against which Thou has had indignation these three score and ten years?

When the Lord replies with comforting words, the angel addresses the prophet, saying:

> Thus saith the Lord: I return to Jerusalem with compassion: My house shall be built in it, saith the

Lord of hosts, and a line will be stretched forth over Jerusalem. Again, proclaim, saying: Thus saith the Lord of hosts. My cities shall again overflow with prosperity; and the Lord shall yet comfort Zion, and shall yet choose Jerusalem. (1:9-17)

In Chapter Three the prophet sees Joshua the high priest standing before the angel of the Lord, and *HaSātān* standing at his right hand to accuse him. But the Lord rebukes *HaSātān*, and Joshua is invested with authority to lead, together with Zerubbabel, in the rebuilding of the wall of Jerusalem.

In Samuel 24, it is the Lord Himself who moves David to carry out a census. But in I Chronicles 21, the opening sentence reads:

And Satan stood up against Israel and incited David to number Israel.

Here for the first time the word Satan appears without the article, which had led commentators to regard it as a proper name, suggesting to them a being with a personality more distinct than in all other scriptural contexts. Some commentators have even proposed a developmental view of the term satan. Rivkah Scharf Kluger, for example, has argued that the word Satan in Chronicles is a proper name and, therefore, closest to the post-biblical view of Satan found in the apocryphal literature of pre-Christian Judaism, in which the dualistic tendency becomes more pronounced.[4] But Peggy L. Day, in an extraordinarily thoughtful study of the term Satan in the Hebrew Bible, rejects Kluger's developmental thesis. Kluger, under the influence of Jungian psychology, had proposed a process of development within the divine personality: a progressive cleansing of Yahweh's "dark side," a goal finally achieved in I Chronicles 21, where Satan is presumably an independent personality. Day, however, challenges the notion that Satan in I

Chronicles 21:1-22:1 should be translated as a proper name. The noun Satan, she argues, can mean both "adversary" in general and "legal accuser" in particular, and

> it was used to refer to various beings, both terrestrial and divine when they played either of these adversarial roles...[Hence] it becomes clear that there is not one celestial *satan* in the Hebrew Bible, but rather the potential for many. And if the *satan* of, for instance, Zechariah 3 is not the same *satan* as the one dispatched to oppose Balaam, nor the one who provoked David to number Israel, then we certainly should not speak of a single developing character or personality.[5]

After examining the biblical evidence Day concludes that there was no *office* of accuser in ancient Israel (39); and that the reason for the definite article in *HaSātān* is unclear. She proposes that

> In heaven as on earth, the term *satan* had neither a single meaning nor a sole referent. And when Satan, as it were, materializes as an independent personality, the traits attributed to him definitely include reflections of and implications drawn from certain of the texts that employ the noun *satan*; but what we might call Satan's fundamental purpose and nature was not derived from any of the biblical *satan* texts. Without the fundamental notion of a semi-autonomous archfiend who wields the forces of evil against God's will and to the detriment of all humankind, there is no Satan. (63)

Day is right, I believe, to reject the developmental thesis; and her analysis helps us recognize that the use of the definite article together with the other characteristics ascribed to "the Satan's" relationship with God, make *HaSātān* of Job a more autonomous personality than Satan of I Chronicles 21, and certainly more offensive.

It is precisely in that regard that Kluger, notwithstanding her developmental thesis and Jungian framework, makes a cogent observation of moment concerning *HaSātān* of Job:

> the *Satan* of the Book of Job stands face to face with God in a dialectical discussion (80)

Although *HaSātān* is, of course, subordinate to God, his considerable power has been overlooked.

> After all, he is able to incite Yahweh to turn against Job, to cause Him to make a momentous decision. Yahweh lets himself become involved in a serious discussion with this demon and be influenced by him. It is true that Yahweh continues to have faith in Job; but, looked at psychologically, is there not, in the very acceptance of the wager, a concession to *HaSātān's* doubt? If there had been no secret uncertainty to rouse His interest in the outcome of this truly immoral wager at the expense of His servant Job, he would most probably have refused to engage in it. (80)

Moreover, Kluger calls attention to the implications of that revealing sentence which the Jobian author placed in the mouth of Yahweh:

> thou didst move Me against him [Job], to destroy him without cause. (Job 2:3)

And Kluger comments convincingly:

> He [Yahweh] accuses *HaSātān* of having seduced Him to an act which He really repents – only to allow Himself to be "incited" by *HaSātān* on a further

> occasion ... It is scarcely possible to regard this as a demonstration of Yahweh's omnipotence. (81)

Kluger continues:

> An old Talmud teacher seems to me to have had a finer sense for the atmosphere of the story than those who belittle the significance of *HaSātān* in this text. He remarks in regard to Chapter 2:3 ("thou movedst me against him, to destroy him without cause"): "If it were not in the Bible, one would not be allowed to say it," for God is represented "like a man who lets Himself be seduced by another." (Kluger, 82)

Kluger also cites the Old Testament scholar Hermann Gunkel who observed that the wager sounds as if it were made not between a servant and a master high above him, but rather as between two equals:

> This impression is also supported by the fact that in this story Yahweh and Satan [sic] speak together without regard for the immeasurable distance between them. (Kluger, 82)

There is general agreement among scholars that it was during the long sojourn of the Judeans among the Persians that certain Zoroastrian ideas influenced the Hebrew faith.[6] The fundamental conception of the Deity as of one formless, incorporeal Almighty God was by that time so firmly implanted in the consciousness of the Judeans, that few failed to see the error of the Iranian doctrine of acknowledging two great, rival powers, Ahura-Mazda (Ormuzd), the god of light and goodness, and Anero-Mainyus (Ahriman), the god of darkness and evil. The Judean spiritual leaders, denying that humankind is perpetually drawn in opposite directions by two rival cosmic powers, underscored the foundational premise of Judaism: God is the creator of all things, including light and darkness.

But although the Judeans resisted any alteration in the conception of their Deity, they could not prevent the absorption of several Persian ideas and customs. They imagined, for instance, that they enhanced the glory of God if, in imitation of the Iranians, they surrounded Him with myriads of obedient servants. The "messengers of God," whom we read about in the Bible as executors of His will, became, after the pattern of Persian beliefs, heavenly creatures endowed with peculiar characteristics and individuality. The people pictured to themselves the divine throne, surrounded by a throng of heavenly beings, or angels, awaiting a sign to do God's bidding. Like the Persians, the Judeans gave the angels special names: Michael, Gabriel, Raphael, Uriel, and others.

As the Judean imagination had transformed the Yazatas into angels, and given them a Hebrew character and Hebrew names, so also were the evil spirits, or Daevas, introduced among the Judeans. Satan was a copy of Anero-Mainyus, but he was not placed in juxtaposition to the God of Israel, for this would, of course, have contradicted the fundamental biblical principle. He, the Holy One, the Almighty, could not be limited by one of His own creatures. In the Hebrew Bible taken as a whole, this principle was carefully preserved; and it was the post-biblical writers who went further and created a full-blown Satan who soon grew to be as powerful as his Iranian prototype. Satan thus acquired a kingdom of darkness of his own, where he reigned as the supreme arbiter of evil. Once created in the image of Anero-Mainyus, Satan had to be surrounded with a host of attendant demons or evil spirits (*Shedim, Mazikim, Malahei Habalah*). One demon, as an adaptation of the Iranian Daeva names, was called *Ashmodai*; another by the name of *Samael*, who was at the head of a troop of persecuting spirits. The angel of death (*Mal'akh Hamawet*), lying in ambush ready to snatch away human life was endowed with a thousand eyes. These creatures of the imagination soon took hold of the Jewish mind and became popular spirits in intertestamental Judaism.

Most scholars would agree, then, that the Persian influence of Ahriman on the figure of Satan may be recognized in post-biblical Judaism and in early Christianity, and that there is no full-blown Satan in the Hebrew Bible. Nevertheless, *HaSātān* in the Book of Job certainly stands out as a uniquely malevolent and despicable member of the *bnei elohim*, capable of inducing God to become an accomplice in the perpetration of evil. In this light, one may suggest that although there is no metaphysical, anti-God being or domain in the Hebrew Bible, the Book of Job is the only text that opened the door, as it were, for the post-biblical writers to take the concept further and turn *HaSātān* into Satan.

Was the Original Jobian Text Modified?

One of the questions that emerges from our critical reflections on the extant text of the Book of Job is whether it is the original, or whether the original was modified and transformed for certain religious and ideological reasons. As Morris Jastrow, Jr. observed many decades ago, everything about the Book of Job is perplexing.[7] The language is difficult and in many places incomprehensible; the organization is complex and the setting is strange; and the original work was most probably transformed in the interest of the conventional orthodoxy of the time. In its original form, Jastrow argues convincingly, the book was the product of a skeptic, challenging the fundamental axiom of the Hebrew prophets, that God governs the universe in accordance with the principles of justice. The original author was a great questioner: Why should the just man suffer? So for the author Job represents "Everyman" as the just sufferer.

Jastrow compares the Book of Job with Ecclesiastes, which addresses similar issues:

> Consider the work of God; for who can make that straight, which He hath made crooked? In the day of prosperity be joyful, and in the day of adversity consider; God hath made even the one as well as the other, to the end that man should find nothing after him.
> All things have I seen in the days of my vanity; there is a righteous man that perisheth in his righteousness, and there is a wicked man that prolongeth his life in his evil-doing. (Eccl.7:13-15)

Jastrow calls Ecclesiastes a gentle cynic who takes things as they are. Not so the author of Job, for whom wickedness has usurped the place of justice. Ecclesiastes says:

> I saw under the sun, in the place of justice, that wickedness was there; and in the place of righteousness, that wickedness was there. (3:16)

But he adds:

> I said in my heart: God will judge the righteous and the wicked; for there is a time there for every purpose and for every work. (3:17)

For the author of Job, however, the conspicuous absence of justice constitutes the central problem of the human condition, raising, as it does, the possibility that the universe is governed by an impersonal and cruel FATE, not a loving father of humankind.

Job's friends, then, are foils against which he can challenge the premises of the prevalent orthodoxy. But, as Jastrow observes in a telling question: Is not the orthodox view triumphant in the end with Job's repentance? For given this ending, the text as it lies before us tends to argue for the maintenance of the traditional doctrine, that justice will prevail. Jastrow's central thesis therefore is that the originally skeptical book was transformed in order to make it acceptable to orthodoxy.

In a careful and objective reading of the text, one can only agree with Jastrow, that the real and original Job engaged in a bold indictment of Divine injustice:

> What an awful deity to permit a man "perfect and removed from evil" (1:2) to be thus wracked on the wheel! The introduction of the scene between Yahweh and Satan [sic] only enhances the callousness of the former in heaping misfortunes on an innocent head, just for the satisfaction of winning a wager. What a shocking and immoral story … (32)

For Jastrow, the problem the author faced was how to reconcile the Yahweh of the story with the conception of God taught by the prophets: a supreme being ruling the world and the destinies of humankind by means of just laws tempered with mercy. That is the issue debated in the exchanges between Job and his friends. Ostensibly, then, the book was written to search for the cause of suffering and evil in a world created by a supposedly just and compassionate, loving creator. To support his view that the existing text has been tendentiously edited and rewritten, Jastrow calls attention to the fact that Job of the story is separated from Job in the exchange with his friends:

> The story of the pious, patient, taciturn Job is told in prose, whereas the other Job who is impatient and rebellious, voluble in the denunciation of the cruel fate meted out to him, and blasphemous in his charges of injustice against the creator of the universe in control of the destinies of mankind is made to speak in poetry, as are his friends. (39)

Moreover, the uncritical tradition fails to discern contradictions such as that between 2:10, which states that Job "sinned not with his lips," and 7:11, where he says,

> Therefore I will not refrain my mouth,
> I will speak in the anguish of my spirit;
> I will complain in the bitterness of my soul.

Jastrow convincingly observes that the real and original Job goes so far as to assert that it is God's nature to take pleasure in seeing the innocent suffer:

> Though I be innocent, He shall prove me perverse.
> I am innocent – I regard not myself, I despise
>   my life.

> It is all one – therefore I say:
> He destroyeth the innocent and the wicked.
> If the scourge slay suddenly,
> *He will mock at the calamity of the guiltless.*
> The earth is given into the hand of the wicked;
> He covereth the faces of the judges thereof;
> If it be not He, who then is it? (9:20-24)

So Jastrow cogently argues that

> The Job of the story has sublime faith in God's justice, despite all appearances to the contrary. The Job of the discussions conceives God as strong and powerful, but as arbitrary and without a sense of justice. Such are the two Jobs, the one as far removed from the other as heaven is from earth. (41)

The friends are at first shocked by Job's extreme suffering; they are even sympathetic, as expressed in their silent commiseration; but in the dialogue, responding to the second Job, their sympathy turns into harsh criticism and even hostility. Bildad asks:

> How long wilt Thou speak these things,
> Seeing that the words of thy mouth are as a mighty wind?
> Doth God pervert judgment?
> Or doth the Almighty pervert justice?
> If thy children sinned against Him,
> He delivered them into the hand of their transgression. (8:2-4)

And Zophar hurls the following at Job: "Know therefore that God exacteth of thee less than thine iniquity deserveth." (11:6)

Two conceptions of the Deity may also be discerned. Yahweh of the story is different from the Elohim in the dialogues:

Yahweh takes pride in Job's piety and expresses full confidence that His servant Job will endure the test to which he has been put at the instigation of *HaSātān*; but all the names for God – *Elohim, El, Eloha, Shadai* – denote a supreme being of universal scope. Job is said to be "greater than any sons of the East," but the absence from the book of both "Israel" and the concept of the "covenant," together with the "land of Uz" east of Palestine, suggest a non-Hebrew origin of the story. In the dialogue between God and *HaSātān*, the name Yahweh is introduced; but Job and his wife use Elohim.

On the question of the name of *HaSātān*, Jastrow observes:

> Satan[sic] in the Prologue ... is a semi-divine being, placed on a par with the "sons of God," although occupying an *independent* position. (54, italics added)

But Jastrow goes on to say that "the Satan" of Job

> has not yet advanced to the position of "accuser," as he appears in Zechariah (3:1-2), but he is on the road to assuming the general role of an enemy of man – the one who tempts man towards evil. (54)

One can agree with the latter part of the statement – that "the Satan" of Job "is on the road to assuming the general role of an enemy of man" – but not with the first part of the statement comparing him favorably with "the Satan" of Zechariah. For as we have demonstrated in our analysis of the several occurrences of the term Satan in the Hebrew Bible, there is no pattern of development reaching its peak in I Chronicles 21:1. And in Zechariah, though the text employs the phrase "to accuse him," the role of *HaSātān* is certainly less malevolent than his role in Job. Indeed, in Zechariah the Lord cuts him short immediately:

> And he showed me Joshua the high priest standing before the angel of the Lord, and *HaSātān* standing at his right hand to accuse him. And the Lord said unto *HaSātān*: "The Lord rebuke thee, O *HaSātān*, yea, the Lord that hath chosen Jerusalem rebuke thee; is not this man a brand plucked out of the fire? (3:1-2)

So the role of "the Satan" of Zechariah has no real consequences. Jastrow, like some other scholars, also wishes to make something of moment out of the difference between II Samuel 24:1 and I Chronicles 21:1. In the earlier, he avers, it is God's anger that prompts David to sin by imposing a census upon the people; whereas when Chronicles came to be compiled in the fourth or third century BCE, God is replaced by Satan, acting apparently *independently*: "And Satan stood up against Israel, and moved David to number Israel." (21:1) Although it is true that Satan appears here to be acting independently, one must emphasize again that where malevolence is concerned, his action is hardly to be compared with that of *HaSātān* in Job. The numbering of the people implies a census for the purpose of taxation; and doubtless, the people, then as now, hated to be taxed. But considered historically, David's census was not necessarily an evil act. As the Hasting's *Dictionary of the Bible* interprets the act,

> The taking of a census, despite popular prejudice against it, was another device on David's part to centralize the authority in himself and break down the old tribal system; and for the same reason he divided the land into districts, because it was apparently he who initiated the practice, although Solomon carried it out in a more sweeping fashion. (see *David*, p. 202)

It is true that an adequate assessment of the consequences of the census would require a careful and objective analysis of the historical context. Short of that, however, one can say that if it was David's aim to unify the country, one ought not assume that this was necessarily a tyrannical act on his part, since David, unlike Solomon after him, is never accused of being a despot. Though David's efforts to preserve the unity of the realm ultimately failed, one may reasonably view those efforts in a positive light:

> Despite all of David's attempts to unify the country, and despite the esteem in which he himself was held, the old rivalries between north and south continued, and there were revolts against him, the most serious of which was led by his own son Absalom. (*Ibid.*)

Jastrow's truly significant contribution is to recognize that there are two Jobs in the text, and that the real Job of the original folk tale is the rebellious one. The sudden and unmistakable change of character that strikes one immediately in 42:2-6, is totally at odds with the earlier Job who cried aloud there is no justice and consistently maintained that it is the Deity who has subverted his cause, compassed him with His net, kindled His wrath against him and counted him as one of His enemies. The conclusion of the extant work in which Job is represented as justified while his friends are rebuked, was added, Jastrow proposes, to the original form; the ending in which Job confesses he was wrong belongs to the book "in a form amplified to controvert the aim of the older book" (63). The word "curse" was also replaced with the word "bless" in 1:5; 1:11; 2:5; and changes were made throughout (additions and deletions) in an effort to weaken the skeptical trend and strengthen the patient, pious and repentant elements. And in that way the transformed text became acceptable to the orthodox, for whom the rebellious and impatient Job represents a passing mood, while the true Job is revealed in his pious utterances.

Some redactors, Jastrow argues, made changes even after the earliest, transformed text had become relatively fixed. Impressed by the book as it stood, but determined to make it a defense of orthodoxy, a redactor could not reconcile himself to the thought that Job could utter such a defiant challenge as:

> Though He slay me, I tremble not [which is the way Jastrow translates, *Hen yikteleini l'o 'ayahel*].

So it was replaced with:

> Though He slay me, yet will I trust in Him. (13:15)

Less convincing, however, is what Jastrow has to say concerning 29:12-16 and 31:5-8. In the former passage Job says of himself:
> Because I delivered the poor that cried,
> The fatherless also, that had none to help him.
> The blessing of him that was ready to perish came upon me;
> And I caused the widow's heart to sing for joy.
> I put on righteousness, and it clothed itself with me;
> My justice was as a robe and a diadem.
> I was eyes to the blind,
> And feet was I to the lame.
> I was a father to the needy;
> And the cause of him that I knew not, I searched out.

And the latter passage reads:

> If I have walked with vanity,
> And my foot hath hasted to deceit –
> Let me be weighed in a just balance,
> That God may know mine integrity –
> If my step hath turned out of the way,

> And my heart walked after mine eyes,
> And if any spot hath cleaved to my hands;
> Then let me sow, and let another eat;
> Yea, let the produce of my field be rooted out.

Jastrow states that the impression of Job the rebel is spoiled by these passages in which he sings "his own praises." It "is difficult to suppose," he writes,

> that the writers of the original book of Job should have allowed their hero thus to lay himself open to the charge of pharisaical [sic] self-esteem and smug self-glorification. This picture of the self-satisfied, boastful Job is due to others ... (138-139)

But Jastrow may be pressing his point too hard here, for both passages and especially the second may be viewed as compatible with the rebellious Job who adamantly protests his innocence and demands a hearing before the Almighty. Furthermore, what Jastrow overlooks in his critique of these passages is that the Lord Himself had averred

> that there is none like him [Job] in the earth, a wholehearted and an upright man, one that feareth God, and shunneth evil. (1:8-9)

So Job is not necessarily smug, self-glorifying and boastful in these passages; he is rather defending and affirming his innocence by recounting some of his *Mizwwt* and demanding that he "be weighed in a just balance."

Jastrow proposes that the primary aim of the original Book of Job is not to deny providence, but to enter a protest against the view that the universe is governed according to the principles of justice and mercy. And Jastrow adds:

> While Israel, the suffering servant of Yahweh, and Job the suffering individual are merely two aspects of one and the same problem, the significant feature of the philosophy in the Book of Job lies, however, in the application of the problem to the individual. (156)

There is, however, another momentous difference between Israel as the suffering servant and Job as the suffering individual. In the biblical narratives dealing with Israel's historical experiences, her suffering is interpreted in terms of the Hebrew Bible's religious and moral framework: if Israel has sinned, she is chastised by the Lord with the aim of teaching her to change her ways. The Book of Job, however, lies outside that framework, as Job suffers frightfully for no good reason whatsoever. The heart of the moral framework is the *berit*, the covenantal relationship. As Max Weber has explained so well: If Yahweh

> was angry and failed to help the nation or the individual, a violation of the *berith* with Him had to be responsible for it. Hence, it was necessary for the [spiritual] authorities as well as for the individual from the outset to ask, which commandment had been violated? Irrational divination means could not answer this question, only knowledge of the very commandments and soul-searching. Thus, the idea of the *berith* flourishing in the truly Yahwistic circles pushed all scrutiny of the divine will toward an at least relatively rational mode of raising and answering the question.[8]

The absence of the *berit* from the Book of Job is therefore no small omission, as I shall emphasize again and again; for it means that Job's soul-searching, and his rational mode of asking why he suffers so, cannot produce a rational answer. In these terms, the Book of Job breaks out of the Bible's theological framework and fails dismally to provide even the vaguest hint as to why the innocent individual suffers.

Jastrow reminds us of the transition in the Hebrew Bible from collective to individual responsibility. In Jeremiah we read:

> In those days they shall say no more:
> "The fathers have eaten sour grapes,
> And the children's teeth are set on edge."
> But everyone shall die for his own iniquity; every man
> that eateth the sour grapes, his teeth shall be set
> on edge. (Jer. 31:29-30)

And the same new conception in Ezekiel:
> Therefore I will judge you, O house of Israel, every one according to his ways, saith the Lord God. Return ye, and turn yourselves from all your transgressions; so shall they not be a stumbling block of iniquity unto you. (Ezek. 18:30)

The Book of Job reflects this transition as Job takes full responsibility for his own individual conduct. Indeed, he takes responsibility, as we have seen, for his children's conduct as well. But the new doctrine seems to have no direct bearing on either Job's plight or the theodicy problem. Jastrow recognizes that the theodicy problem had to be solved – if it were to be solved at all – in this world, since the doctrine of retribution in a future world emerged much later. But if "theodicy" refers to a defense of God's goodness and omnipotence in view of the existence of evil, then we have to say that the theodicy problem is not addressed at all in the book, since though God is described as Almighty, he certainly is not good. An alternative interpretation, equally distasteful, is that the theodicy problem is "solved" by means of a *deus ex machina* named *HaSātān*, who

43

though he is less than a full-blown Satan, nevertheless possesses the ability to cause God to collaborate in perpetrating evil – which tends to contradict His omnipotence.

Jastrow agrees that there is not the faintest suggestion in the Book of Job of an after-life solution to the theodicy problem. The Gehenna, as a place of punishment for the wicked, lay in the future. He also rejects Horace Kallen's thesis, that the Book of Job is based on the model of a Greek tragedy, and that the idea of writing a Jewish drama was suggested to a Jewish writer by having witnessed the production of a play by Euripides in some Greek city. Jastrow agrees with most scholars that there is no need to posit Greek or Hellenistic influence on the book. The fact that the book neither provides nor attempts to provide a *rational* solution to the theodicy problem speaks against a Greek influence. Jastrow claims, surprisingly in the light of his own analysis, that in the Book of Job "faith rises superior to argument and speculation" (192). But one must ask: faith? Where in the book does Jastrow find faith, after and in spite of his demonstration that the text has been thoroughly tampered with?

Jastrow, like other outstanding commentators whom we shall soon also engage in dialogue, concludes his commentary with the proposition that there is design in the world, though man cannot fathom the mystery of his life, which entails suffering without apparent justification, and guilt that goes unpunished. Notwithstanding the strictures we have leveled against the Book of Job, Jastrow nonetheless insists – again surprisingly – that the spirit of the book is "genuinely Hebraic." But to that we would have to reply: In what sense? And how would Jastrow propose that we derive consolation from its so-called "Hebraic" message?

The Book of Job: Its Idiosyncrasies

Most, if not all, commentators on the Book of Job recognize its idiosyncrasies and its theologically offensive elements; but they strive nevertheless to provide some kind of theological apologia for the book. We have seen this attempt to present the book's message in a positive light in the commentary of Driver and Gray, and in that of Jastrow; and we will continue to see this tendency by several other commentators whom we engage in a critical dialogue.

John E. Hartley, for example, states that

> the Yahweh speeches present several perplexing problems ... *on the surface* they fail to address the issue of the suffering righteous, and they skirt Job's complaint that God fails to keep times of judgment. (24:1-17) Amazingly, they seem to ignore Job's avowal of innocence, for Yahweh neither condemns Job nor acquits him. Moreover, modern readers in search of insight into the issue of suffering are often keenly disappointed with the Yahweh speeches.[9]

One wonders why Hartley says only "on the surface." In God's speech to Job He asserts that He has structured the world exactly according to His blueprints (38:4-8). No corner of the world is outside His authority (38:16-24). He wisely orders the heavenly elements and cares for the wild animals (38:25-39:30). Does this also imply, Hartley asks, "that He certainly watches over people just as wisely and caringly," as some interpretations have suggested? And Hartley replies:

> [In] questioning Job so intently about the created order and the creatures Behemoth and Leviathan, symbols of

hostile cosmic forces, God brings Job to realize that no human being has a proper perspective to justify the course of matters in the universe, let alone to accuse God of acting unjustly.

The foundation of God's argument in His speeches is that power and wisdom are one in the supreme ruler of the universe. (49)

But Job had never doubted the power and wisdom of the supreme ruler; what he asked for was a fair hearing. And if justice is not an essential attribute of the Almighty, does not such a characterization fly in the face of the fundamental premise of the Bible, that He is an ethical Deity? And does not such a characterization tear asunder the covenantal relationship between God and humanity? Yet for Hartley,

the book of Job teaches that a person may serve God faithfully, whether his circumstances are bleak or filled with promise, *for he has to assume that God is for him, seeking his ultimate good*. A person can triumph over suffering through faith in God. (50, italics added)

Where in the Book of Job is there the faintest hint that his peculiar Deity seeks the "ultimate good" of human beings? Let us remind ourselves that we are discussing a definite text; and in that text the Deity not only fails to seek the good for Job, He collaborates in bringing evil upon him. One can understand the role of "faith" in the context of the covenantal relationship. But what role can faith possibly have if, as in the Book of Job, no such relationship exists, and the Deity appears to care not at all for the unjust suffering of a human being. Let us remember too, that the so-called Prologue is an integral part of the Book of Job, and that the source or cause of Job's afflictions was not some sort of impersonal, natural force.

What, therefore, does the nature of the Jobian Deity imply for personal religion – for individuals who appeal to God in prayer, seeking His help?

Hartley proposes that

> By questioning Job about the primordial monsters Behemoth and Leviathan, Yahweh is trying to persuade Job that He is Master of all powers in the world, both earthly and cosmic ... He is Master of all forces ... that brought on Job's affliction. Therefore, if Job is to find favor again, he must submit to Yahweh as his Lord by relinquishing his avowal of innocence[why] and by conceding his complaints against Yahweh's just governance of the world. Yahweh is thus calling Job to decide whether to argue his case and lose, or submit to Yahweh, accepting in trust the blessing and the curse, the riches and the ash-heap. (534)

What kind of theology is this? Hartley describes the relationship between Job and God as if it were a contest, a test of strength. Why should an innocent man give up his avowal of innocence? And why should Job "decide whether to argue his case and lose, or submit to Yahweh?" In the context of the Book of Job as it lies before us, it can only be said that Job is right in arguing his case, for we all know the true cause of the catastrophe that befell him. And why should one accept the "ash-heap" if it is brought on by an evil deed?

Equally problematic in my judgment, are the subsequent propositions on the same page:

> Yahweh raises the key question for Job. Does he have to argue that Yahweh is guilty of governing the world unjustly in order to prove his own innocence? (534)

But that is not at all what Job is after; he wants only to argue his own case, and to persuade God of his own innocence. It is in response to his friends and false comforters, not in response to God, that Job calls attention to the prosperity of the wicked, and challenges the traditional doctrine of retribution. Moreover, in calling attention to the fact that the righteous suffer and the wicked prosper, Job is not impugning the justice of the Deity, for He is no puppeteer, after all, and we are not marionettes. Injustice in the human realm is not the fault of God, but the fault of human beings who have failed to establish just political regimes based on God's ethical commandments.

> If Job thinks Yahweh fails to rule the universe justly, then he is setting himself up as wiser than God, even as one who could rule better than God. (*Ibid.*)

Well, although Job never even implies any such thing, one can say that the author of the Book of Job has given us a conception of God in which He has in fact failed to rule justly: He allowed Himself to be seduced by Job's hateful adversary, and therefore bears responsibility for the *crimes* committed not only against Job, but against all those innocents who perished as a consequence of His "wager."

> Yahweh thus exhorts Job to prove his claims by adorning himself in regal apparel and punishing the wicked. And Yahweh challenges him to show his mastery over the great primordial monsters, Behemoth and Leviathan, which are symbolic of cosmic forces[?] that at times are hostile to Yahweh's rule. (*Ibid.*)

It is a preposterous exhortation that the Jobian author has placed in the mouth of Yahweh. Job never doubted nor challenged God's powers, and certainly never claimed that he, more effectively than Yahweh, could punish the wicked. And in Chapter One of the present essay we have already discussed the symbolic significance of Behemoth and Leviathan, showing that the notion of *cosmic* forces hostile to Yahweh's rule, is foreign to the Hebrew Bible.

> But if Job cannot subdue them [Behemoth and Leviathan], he is in no position to discredit God, his Creator and Master for treating him unjustly. (*Ibid.*)

That statement certainly is a *non-sequitur*! Does Hartley seriously propose that because a human being possesses none of God's powers, he may not ask and expect justice from the Almighty?

> Furthermore, the only conclusion he can come to is that Yahweh is the supreme Lord of the universe. (*Ibid.*)

That is a fact Job never questioned and knew all along. But again, at the risk of belaboring the point, that only proves God's power, not His justice. However, the Jobian author has portrayed the Deity, perhaps inadvertently, as less than omnipotent, since He allowed Himself to be manipulated by a wicked subordinate.

> This means that all creatures must fear Him. (*Ibid.*)

But outside the Book of Job, the highest principles of Yahweh and His prophets teach us to fear Him not simply because He is Almighty; but rather to fear Him when we violate His ethical injunctions, or even contemplate doing so.

> Filled with wonder and awe at Yahweh's appearing, Job confesses his unworthiness. (537)

Why "unworthiness?" Powerlessness yes, but why "unworthiness?" Does Hartley want us to believe that what God demands of us is a recognition and acknowledgement of our unworthiness?

> His [Job's] attention shifts from his concern for vindication to his need to prepare his heart before God. (537)

But if we assume for the moment that the Jobian text had not been transformed in the way Jastrow has argued, we may ask the following question: Had Job known the true cause of his calamity, would he have prepared his heart before God?

> He humbles himself before God because communion with God is more important to him than release from affliction. (*Ibid.*)

Job desired communion with God not for its own sake, but precisely for the sake of removing his afflictions by proving his innocence. And if this bizarre Deity had been less concerned with boasting of His Almightiness, and more concerned with justice, His voice out of the whirlwind would have acknowledged His egregious error.

> It has not been wrong for him to complain, even against God Himself. Nor has it been wrong for him to swear an oath of innocence. But the zealous pursuit of a right eventually erects a barrier between God and the offended person. (*Ibid.*)

The zealous pursuit of a right by an offended person is liable to erect a barrier between him and another person – especially a person whom one loves. But why should the zealous pursuit of a right erect a barrier between an individual and God? -- particularly in a case such as the one before us, in which God Himself was responsible for a wrong. Job was righteous, not self-righteous. Where is the God of justice, for Hartley? Is the following theological message one to which we would wish to subscribe?

> Therefore, when God makes Himself known, the supplicant must surrender everything to God, including his just grievance[?], if he is to avoid sinning and to find God's favor again. (*Ibid.*)

Why is it a sin to press a just grievance? Again, we are talking about the text as it lies before us. Job did not know the true cause of his calamity. What would he have done, however, had he known? Would he have continued to trust in a God who had deferred to *HaSātān*?

> Thus Job renounces all personal claims that could be construed to put himself above God. (*Ibid.*)

One can only respond by reminding Hartley that such a thought never entered Job's mind. Job did not challenge God's power; he questioned God's justice in his own case, and he was right to do so. Indeed, if anyone slyly sought to put himself above God, it was *HaSātān* who successfully drove a wedge between God's power and His justice.

> … Yahweh shows that He permits far more latitude in genuine human searching than that tolerated by those who hold rigidly to a narrow theology. (540)

Let us note, however, that the so-called "latitude in genuine human searching" did not include Job's discovery of the truth.

As one reads Hartley's conclusion, one can only wonder how he could have arrived at it on the basis of the actual Jobian text:

> In the framework of the whole book, Yahweh is the giver of life and blessing, not a capricious tyrant who takes pleasure in the suffering of those who serve Him merely to test their loyalty. Yahweh may withdraw His favor for a season, but His love is for a lifetime. (544-45)

The Book of Job: A Failure

In a similar effort at presenting the Book of Job's message in a positive light, H. Harold Kent proposes that the book "reveals ... the essential nature of true faith."[10] Kent acknowledges that the book is a failure insofar as it fails to explain to anyone's satisfaction why the godly suffer. However, he then goes on to argue that the relationship between God and man in the book

> is shown to be a relationship of grace, which is apprehended by faith, a faith that works in obedience and trust. (13)

Grace? Where is there an act of grace on the part of the Deity in the Book of Job? Let us note the nature of Yahweh's original act of grace in Exodus and Deuteronomy. It was out of His grace, and not any special virtue of the Israelites, that He responded to their cries of oppression. Here we understand clearly what is meant by the gracious act of an ethical Deity who protects the weak from the strong. Hence, the historical experience of the Hebrews taught them that God's grace can be apprehended by faith that He will come to their aid again if, in accordance with the covenant, they obey His ethical commandments. But what can grace apprehended by faith possibly mean in the Jobian context?

Job, Kent observes, asks, if God is just, why does this happen to me? If He is all-powerful, why does He not do something about my case? And Kent replies that the secret of Job's problem

> is that while he believed and hoped and longed, it was not in God but in his own concept of God. (25)

Kent dislikes Job's conduct in which he made himself the judge of his Creator, wanting to tell God how He ought to run our lives. Kent dislikes even the tone of Job's talk with God:

You are unfair. You are wrong, you are a coward. I am not guilty and yet you punish me. (27)

For such conduct Kent accuses Job of displaying a sanctimonious, self-righteous attitude in which he makes God directly responsible for his plight. Well, wasn't Job in fact justified in making the Jobian Deity responsible for his plight? He certainly was on the basis of the text as it stands. Then why call Job "sanctimonious" and "self-righteous"? If the Jobian author had wished to address the question of why the righteous suffer, but without making the Deity responsible for that phenomenon, he should not have written the Prologue.

In several commentaries we encounter the view that the Book of Job's central question is whether human beings can have a *disinterested* love and faith in God. Gustavo Gutiérrez opens his commentary with this question: Can human beings believe in God without looking for rewards and fearing punishments? Are human beings capable, in the midst of unjust suffering, of continuing to maintain their faith in God without expecting a return? For Gutiérrez, it is Satan[sic] and all those who have a barter conception of religion who deny the possibility; whereas the author of the Book of Job, in contrast, believes it to be possible, and Job is his spokesman. For Gutiérrez, "disinterested religion alone is true religion."[11]

In all his suffering, says Gutiérrez, Job refuses to deny God. Yes, of course! Job was no atheist, nor even a skeptic. He believed, in opposition to the proto-Nietzscheans of his time, that God lives! Indeed, so strong was his belief that a just and almighty God lives, that he strove unrelentingly to gain a fair hearing before Him. But what would Job have thought, and how would he have conducted himself, had he learned the true cause of his calamity? We need again to remind ourselves that the cause of Job's tragedy was not rooted in the natural order of things: his children, his servants and his livestock did not die natural deaths, due to the inexorable workings of an amoral cosmos. If Job's afflictions and the loss of his beloved children had in fact been the result of amoral, natural processes, such phenomena would still constitute a theological problem, which needs to be addressed and which we intend to address in the final part of this essay. In the Book of Job, however, the cause of Job's catastrophe is made quite plain in the author's Prologue, which is *one* of our primary reasons for disliking the book and repudiating its message. Gutiérrez asserts that

> In Job the choice is between a religion based on the rights and obligations of human beings as moral agents, and a disinterested belief based on the gratuitousness of God's love. (15)

One must, however, ask what that is supposed to mean. Gutiérrez seems to be putting down the covenantal relationship by calling it a "barter" conception of religion. But what kind of religion is it that would fail to include the "rights and obligations of human beings as moral agents?" Does Gutiérrez reject the covenant? If so, does he not realize that it is *the* source of our knowledge of the difference between right and wrong, good and evil? *Where else would Gutiérrez find the solid ground upon which to base his defense of the poor, the oppressed and the weak, if not from the covenant and the revelation to the prophets and the people of the eternally valid ethical principles?*

It appears, therefore, that when Gutiérrez concludes his commentary with the following statement, he can offer us nothing affirmative with which to replace his so-called "barter" conception of religion:

> Job shows us a way with his vigorous protest ... his facing up to God, and his acknowledgement of the gratuitousness that characterizes God's plan for human history. (102)

Does Gutiérrez not recognize that his so-called "gratuitousness that characterizes God's plan for human history," is equivalent to the atheistic existentialist's view of the human condition? Does Gutiérrez refuse to see that the gratuitousness he ascribes to the Deity left Job with nothing beyond surrender to a heartless cosmic power? The atheist may ascribe gratuitousness (chaos?) to the workings of the cosmos and the human condition; but Gutiérrez ascribes such meaninglessness to God's plan. Why? Is Gutiérrez presenting us with a philosophy of the absurd?

For that is what Dermot Cox presents us with in his commentary on the Book of Job – a study of the absurd. Cox's work is so thoughtfully challenging that it deserves to be cited at length. He notes that Eliphaz in Chapter Four tries to console Job by speaking of God's presence in the face of adversity. For Eliphaz,

> this presence serves as a call to repentance and a hope of rehabilitation. But this very consolation makes things worse for Job. He is *not* a sinner, there can be no question of repentance. His suffering [from his own standpoint] is totally unexplainable, and so God's presence can only be seen as a vindictive torturer playing a particularly savage game of cat-and-mouse with His creature. Since the friends cannot understand this, their presence serves only to drive Job further into isolation.[12]

Job is overcome by terror at his powerlessness, and no effort of his own can lift him out of the absurd. Like Joseph K. in Kafka's *The Trial*, Cox observes, "Job feels he is on trial, a condition made all the more intolerable by the fact that he has no idea of what the charge against him can be and is thus unable to defend himself." (75)

> Yet it is not a question of only one adversary, however powerful … false witnesses harass and malign him … Job's very appearance, his very sufferings, are brought in

> as evidence against him, to prove that he must be evil and in the wrong.
>
> However, the real ground of his anguish ... is the impossibility of finding the judge. This judge is in fact an accusing judge, at once adversary and judge – a travesty of justice. God sees the innocence of the defendant yet refuses to acquit him ... Not only does he allow this perversion of justice – he encourages it. (16:6-11; 19:66ff) Yet Job persists in calling for a hearing from the same judge ... What is the basis of this seemingly contradictory attitude? It can only be due to the conflict between faith and experience. Job has a non-experiential, inherited tradition that since God is just there must be reason in existence, some order or law. This is the residue of man's most primitive thinking, and it is radically contradicted by his personal experience. (76-77)

Cox proceeds to underscore the role of Job's friends who only serve to aggravate his condition. "Insufferable," however,

> as these witnesses are, God is worse. Throughout, Job has described God's hostility in terms of a wild animal savaging his prey. In the second cycle the image changes, and God is seen as far more malignant – he is an unjust judge who distorts justice. (93)

Thus Cox admirably captures the spirit of the Jobian drama, including the repulsive character that the author has ascribed to the Deity. But then Cox spoils the effect of his analysis by striving to present the book's message in a positive theological light. Cox asserts that Job's revolt, his rebellious attitude, is a

> form of atheism, because it subjects God to human judgment, treating him in effect as an equal. (100)

Furthermore, Cox writes

> To declare that God should or should not act in a way conformable to human reason is to equate man and God. (112)

That statement is hard to take seriously. When Abraham argued with God, was he engaging in a form of atheism, equating himself with God? At no point in the Hebrew Bible does the use of reason in the covenantal relationship suggest that in the human employment of reason one presumes to equate oneself with God. Cox doubtless understands this, for in his discussion of Chapter 40:8 and the meaning of *tizdak*, he states that the substantive *zdākāh* expresses the concept of relationship, and can be understood properly only in relation to some sort of contract or covenant:

> with reference to God [Cox writes] the word *zdākāh* is frequently associated with a theophany, where Yahweh reveals himself and his loyalty to his own covenant (137).

One can hardly say it better; so Cox should recognize that the Deity of Job has in fact been disloyal to His own covenant, by which I mean to the covenant of the Hebrew Bible, for there is no covenantal relationship in the Book of Job. Furthermore, although Cox continues to describe the covenantal idea with extraordinary skill, his description remains problematic:

> In fact "righteousness" in the Old Testament is conditioned by this covenantal element and by God's fidelity to the commitments he had already taken. Thus ... *zdākāh* is not so much an attribute of God, as a manifestation of the divine being in his relationship with man and the world. These manifestations are situated in

> a temporal context, God being seen in history as the God of history. *He is just then, not insofar as he acts impartially according to a set norm, but insofar as he follows a constant mode of action in his dealing with the world, in order to realize a definite plan.* (138, italics added)

The underscored passage is certainly not only problematic, but also misleading where the role of God in the covenant is concerned. Is Cox suggesting that there is no explicit and set norm in the covenantal relationship? Is he arguing that when Yahweh came to the aid of the Semitic nobodies in the house of bondage, He was not motivated by a concern with justice? If we take literally what Cox is saying in the underscored passage, he reduces justice to consistency. Does Cox really mean that God is "just" when He "follows a constant mode of action in his dealings with the world, in order to realize a definite plan?" Does Cox mean any "constant mode of action" and any "definite plan?" Or to be accurate and faithful to the meaning of the covenant in the Hebrew Bible, is it not necessary to insist that justice is an essential attribute of God *and* a manifestation of His being in His relationship with humanity and the world?

It is disappointing that Cox strives to defend the Book of Job as a study in the tradition of the absurd. For Cox, what the Jobian Deity was saying in the whirlwind is this:

> Man can be righteous in two ways: by keeping the commandments and the covenant, which is the common level of righteousness; and on a higher level[?] by rejoicing in the will of Yahweh, *whatever that may involve for him*[?], and by recognizing that there is a divine purpose in human affairs and allowing the divine will to become the motivation of one's life [How do we learn of it?] ... Job was just insofar as he lived at the first level, but he lacked an adequate understanding of the implications of righteousness. (143, italics added)

This gloss not only finds no warrant in the Job text, it suggests that as Job's righteousness was at a so-called lower level, he deserved what had befallen him. When Cox describes the higher level as "rejoicing in the will of Yahweh whatever that may involve," can he explain how one is to determine whether an event or chain of events is due to the will of Yahweh and not due to the workings of FATE – the Greek *Moira*? If we accept the premise of the Hebrew Bible, that justice in human relations is the will of Yahweh, then we have a definite guide to action and motivation; but if we assume that the divine will is a mystery, or that anything and everything that transpires is divinely ordained, we have nullified the ethical Deity of the Hebrew Bible and replaced Him with impersonal fate or, indeed, with the absurdity of it all.

It is one thing to propose, as does Cox and certain notable, modern philosophers, that much of human existence appears to be absurd. It is quite another, however, to suggest that the absurdity of human existence is the intended message of the Jobian drama. We must stick to the text; and the text tells us *not* that Job and his loved ones were victims of an absurd natural disaster, nor of human folly or accident. The text tells us that Job and his loved ones were the victims of a conspiracy between the Deity and *HaSātān*. That, together with the other idiosyncrasies of the Book of Job, is what compels us to dislike and repudiate it. When Cox says that

> Job, even in the darkness of the absurd, is free to make an act of faith in Yahweh's control of affairs, (144)

we must remind him that Job was not in the darkness of the "absurd," he was in the dark as to the true cause of the unspeakable crime that was perpetrated against him *and his wife*. Cox, intent upon forcing Job into the tradition of the absurd, asserts that

> Job is being asked in effect by God just what it was that had led him to expect to find reason at the center of existence. (147)

But Job was not expecting to find reason, in the Greek sense, at the center of existence; he was expecting to find reason in the Hebrew sense, of the kind one finds in Isaiah 1:18: "Come now, and let us reason together, saith the Lord." It is reason as an element of the covenantal relationship in which God's justice is presupposed throughout. But Cox's last thoughts are totally at odds with this understanding of the covenantal God:

> The world as experienced by man is irrational, and God is arbitrary, just as Job had been urging in the face of his friend's pious horror. But there is something beyond man's experience that he is not able to judge. The world is not answerable to him. If he believes in a God, the world is answerable only to the creator, who establishes his order, not man's. Alone he created it, alone he judges it. Man must accept that he is part of a pattern he will never comprehend because it is bigger than himself. Even that which is stupid and cruel, even the vagaries of a profligate nature, are only parts of a total pattern, and may only have meaning (if meaning they have) on the level of that pattern. (151)

There can be no doubt that Cox's reflections are the products of a superior mind at work; but however thoughtful his reflections might be, they simply do not speak to the issues raised by the Job text. They speak, instead, to what is perhaps the modern man's sense of the meaninglessness of it all and his attendant malaise. Moreover, the preceding passage as well as the following one from Cox's commentary, might more easily fit into a philosophy of resignation to fate, than a philosophy derived from a belief in the God of the Hebrew prophets: The answer, then," Cox concludes,

> would seem to be the stupendous unreason of it all. The absence of any answer is the only possible answer – for it forces man into the only possible authentic position, the recognition of reality. It is better to see that there is no answer than to build one's existence on a false answer. No amount of "righteousness," no amount of suffering can give a man a right to question absurdity, he must accept it. In this acceptance he will have a firm basis on which to build an authentic relationship with his world. Yahweh is not a God who takes away pain, or who carefully correlates the elements of existence so as to exhibit a pattern. He is essentially the "something outside" that gives meaning to an absurd existence by the hope that there is an ultimate meaning, an ultimate plan. (153)

It seems that Cox has opted for the amoral Jobian Deity over the ethical Deity of the covenant. As a result, Cox's philosophy also lacks an ethical foundation on which to build decent human relations and just political regimes. In those terms, nihilism is perhaps not too harsh an epithet with which to characterize Cox's outlook on life as expressed in his Commentary. However, his powerful formulation of the absurdity of it all challenges us to provide an affirmative alternative to the tradition of the absurd. That is what we hope to accomplish in the final part of this essay. First, however, we need to consider a few more brilliant and challenging commentaries.

Additional Profound and Challenging Commentaries

Samuel Terrien's commentary on the Book of Job is certainly one of the most profound and challenging. He writes that the book

> punctures traditional beliefs in God, but not in faith ... It lifts man from the plight of meaningless existence by inserting him into the context of the *Opus Dei*. It points to a God beyond the God of ethical concept ... It offers a theology of creative participation.[13]

Job's poet, Terrien continues, asks for faith in a Deity

> who transcends all human interests and even morality. (20) The poet of Job did not attempt to solve the problem of evil nor did he propose a vindication of God's justice. For him, any attempt of man to justify God would have been an act of arrogance. (21)

Right at the outset, then, Terrien makes assertions that need to be questioned in the light of the critique of the Book of Job we have offered so far: a "God beyond the God of ethical concept?" A Deity "who transcends all human interests and even morality?" What kind of God is that? If He transcends human needs and concerns, why would human beings need such a God? And if God gave Job and all human beings reason and intelligence, why does Job's call for a fair hearing constitute arrogance?

Terrien acknowledges that

> From the standpoint of Hebrew-Christian orthodoxy, the poem was highly offensive, and it was preserved only because its prose framework upheld the orthodox

> doctrine of divine retribution … Job may have spoken rashly in the poem, but he repented and the Lord rewarded[?] him in the end. (24)

Terrien further acknowledges that

> one cannot help being disturbed by the theological implications of the story. What kind of divine being is portrayed here? For the sake of winning a wager over a cynic in the heavenly council, … the Deity allows that his best servant be brought to destitution and torture. (25)

Nevertheless, Terrien, like all commentators, defends the book's message.

The primary aim of the book, he avers, was to raise the issue of "selfless piety,"

> It did not ask the question, "Why does God permit undeserved suffering?" Rather, it reflected on the query, "Is there among men an exquisite love of God which is not a calculating love?" The story showed itself to be at once naively optimistic and yet pessimistic, for it answered, "Yes, there is such a love among men, but quite exceptionally so. Once upon a time there lived a man in the land of Uz …" (30)

Yes, Job was exceptionally righteous and devout, which makes his undeserved catastrophe all the more outrageous. Do we need, however, to assume that an exquisite love of God must be an uncalculating love? Was Job's own love of God totally uncalculating? We have seen in Chapter One that following the feasts that Job's sons were accustomed to hold with their sisters, Job

> sent and sanctified them, and rose up early in the morning, and offered burnt-offerings according to the number of them all; for Job said: "It may be that my sons have sinned, and blasphemed God in their hearts." Thus did Job [continually] all of his days. (1:4-5)

Out of fear that his loved ones may have entertained impious or impure thoughts, Job, holding himself responsible for his children's conduct, *prudently* propitiates the Almighty; and he does so as a matter of course. Apparently even Job's love of God was not entirely a selfless, disinterested love. Indeed, one must question whether there can be any such thing in the human condition as a disinterested love of God. And one must also question the proposition that an "interested" love of God is somehow a lower order of love. Is not a so-called disinterested love of God a condition of which we are incapable as frail, vulnerable and anxious human beings? Furthermore, as Terrien well knows, the demand for such a love is simply not to be found in the covenant theology of the Hebrew Bible. Nor to be found in the theology of either post-biblical Judaism or that of the New Testament – where it was in the hope of salvation that one impatiently awaited Messianic redemption and the Kingdom of Heaven on earth.

As William James sagely observed in his *The Varieties of Religious Experience*,

> Life and its negations are beaten up inextricably together. But if the life be good, the negation of it must be bad. Yet the two are equally essential facts of existence; and all natural happiness seems infected with a contradiction. The breath of the sepulchre surrounds it.[14]

And James continues:

> the fact that we *can* die, that we *can* be ill at all, is what perplexes us; the fact that we now for a moment live and are well is irrelevant to that perplexity. We need a life not correlated with death, a health not liable to illness, a kind of good that will not perish, a good in fact that lies beyond the goods of nature. (*Ibid.*)

As James therefore recognized,

> Here is the real core of the religious problem. Help! Help! (139)

What James had to say about the religious experience cannot be shrugged off as cynical psychology. If we stop to reflect on the world-religions, we will readily see that in each and every one of them a salvational element – a cry for help – is salient and fundamental. And that is certainly undeniable where Judaism and Christianity are concerned.

Even if we limit ourselves to the Book of Deuteronomy, it is altogether clear that from the very beginning of the Hebrew faith God's revelation posited an explicitly covenantal relationship, an understanding of mutual obligation: If Yahweh liberates the people and teaches them the difference between right and wrong, the people must live in accordance with God's ethical commandments if they wish to prosper. The Lord, through His prophet Moses, commanded the people to observe the Ten Commandments now and forever. We call the God of the Hebrew Bible an ethical Deity because the love and devotion He demanded was the keeping of His commandments. Invariably accompanying God's demand was a promise that if the people will always revere Him and follow all of His commandments, then it will go well with them and their children forever (Deut.

5:26). Moses dinned it into the people's ears, that they should observe the laws which the Lord had enjoined upon them, to the end that they may long endure:

> Obey, O Israel, willingly and faithfully, that it may go well with you and that you may increase greatly [in] a land flowing with milk and honey ... (Deut. 6:3)

This strongly suggests that the love of God cannot be separated or even distinguished from obedience to His ethical commandments; and that a so-called "disinterested" love of God was not required.

It was, of course, strictly out of God's grace that he chose those Semitic nobodies as His treasured people. It was not for any special virtues that He chose them, but rather because He had heard their cries of oppression that He decided to rescue them from the house of bondage. Understood throughout is that God graciously offered the people a covenant: *If* the people will obey His rules and observe them faithfully, then "He will love you and bless you and multiply you." The reward for their faithful observance is explicit, concrete, detailed and in this world: the Lord will

> bless the issue of your womb and the produce of your soil, your new grain and wine and oil, the calving of your herd and the lambing of your flock ... (7:12)

Moses reminds the people repeatedly that they must not say to themselves that the Lord their God will enable them to occupy the promised land for any supposed virtues on their part:

> It is not because of your virtues and your rectitude that you will be able to occupy their country ... Know, then, that it is not for any virtue of yours that the Lord your God is giving you this good land to occupy; for you are a stiffnecked people. (9:4-6)

In the religious and moral framework of the Scriptures, it is therefore understood that between the Lord and the people there are reciprocal obligations. Yes, the people will possess a land with streams and springs and fountains; a land of wheat and barley, vines, figs and pomegranates, a land of olive-trees and honey; *but* the people must fulfill their part of the bargain or risk losing it all. For the Lord has endowed them with the freedom of choice:

> See, this day I set before you blessing and curse: blessing, if you obey the commandments of the Lord your God which I enjoin upon you this day; and curse, if you do not obey the commandments of the Lord your God, but turn away from the path which I enjoin upon you this day ... (11:26-28)

I am fully aware that Terrien knows all this and that for him and, perhaps, the reader I am belaboring the obvious. But how, otherwise, can I make the point that there does not seem to be any "disinterestedness," in Terrien's sense, in the covenant theology of the Pentateuch.

Neither were the demands of the prophets of social justice a call for a disinterested love of God. Only if the princes ceased to oppress the people, and the people ceased to worship objects of wood and stone fashioned by their hands – idols that were no-gods – would the Lord cease to chastise them. Hence, loving God with all of one's heart and soul could not be separated from observing His Commandments and heeding His ordinances and holding fast to them. Evil came not from some metaphysical, autonomous domain, but from disloyalty to God, of which the chief if not sole criterion was disobedience to His Commandments. Although the socio-moral virtues became paramount with the Eighth-Century prophets – Amos, Hosea, Isaiah, Micah – the concern for the poor, the needy and the weak had already come to the fore in the ideals of the Pentateuch: the injunction to practice the remission of debts every seventh year, to open one's hand and lend the needy sufficient for what they need; to free the Hebrew slave in the seventh year of his or her service; and when freeing a slave, to furnish him with the material means of sustaining his freedom. The people are continually urged to bear in mind that they were slaves in Egypt, and should therefore understand in the marrow of their bones what it means to be oppressed. As a formerly enslaved people, Israel, above all, should know how to conduct themselves justly in their relations with their fellow humans.

There is nothing esoteric in God's Commandments. Readily understandable, there is nothing in them that even a young child can fail to grasp. No one can therefore rightfully claim that the Lord's *Torah*, or Instruction, is mysterious, baffling or incomprehensible. It seems clear, then, that in accordance with the covenantal principle, one's love of God must manifest itself in the faithful obedience to His Commandments, and that it is in one's *interest*, both as an individual and as a member of society, to show one's love of God by obeying Him.

Now if I have presented the premises of the covenantal relationship at length, it is for two reasons. The first is that I intend in the concluding portion of this essay to argue that far from being obsolete, defunct or superseded, the covenant must serve as the foundation of our religious, moral and social life. The second reason is to underscore the consequences of the glaring omission of the covenantal relationship from the Book of Job. The Israelites, we are told, possessed no special virtues, and yet God heard their cries and graciously responded. Job, in contrast, was special, as the Lord Himself testified:

> There is none like him in the earth, a wholehearted and an upright man, one that fears God, and shuns evil. (1:8-9)

And yet, when the Lord finally speaks out of the whirlwind to this especially virtuous man, He responds ungraciously, to say the least:

> Who is this who darkens counsel
> By words without knowledge? (38:1)

Let us also note with regard to Terrien's "disinterested" thesis, that in the Lord's words 1:8-9, it is said that Job *fears* God – which suggests something more than a disinterested love of God.

Before we leave this aspect of Terrien's thesis, we need to address this question: Is the love of God taught in the New Testament any more disinterested than that taught in the Hebrew Bible? We read in Matthew that soon after Jesus had heard that John the Baptist was cast into prison, he began to preach and say, "Repent: for the kingdom of heaven is at hand" (Matt.4:17). And when the multitudes of people followed him, he went up into a mountain and there taught his disciples what have come to be called the Beatitudes. Clearly, the promise of the kingdom, in and of itself, constituted for the pious and repentant the expectation that they will receive an extraordinary reward. The Beatitudes are explicit in that regard:

> Blessed are the poor, for theirs is the kingdom of heaven. Blessed are the meek, for they shall inherit the earth. Blessed are they who hunger and thirst after righteousness, for they shall be filled. Blessed are the merciful, for they shall obtain mercy. Blessed are the pure in heart, for they shall see God. Blessed are the peacemakers, for they shall be called the children of God. Blessed are they who are persecuted for righteousness sake; for theirs is the kingdom of heaven ... Rejoice and be exceedingly glad, for great is your reward in heaven.

And when Jesus avers that he has come not to destroy the law or the prophets, he warns and promises that whoever

> shall break one of these least commandments, and shall teach men so, he shall be called the least in the kingdom of heaven; but whosoever shall do and teach them, the same shall be called great in the kingdom of heaven. (5:17-19)

In Matthew, Chapters Six and Seven, we continue to hear utterances attributed to Jesus promising reward: Give alms anonymously,

> otherwise ye have no reward of your Father who is in heaven. (6:1)
>
> If ye forgive men their trespasses, your heavenly Father will also forgive you. (6:14)
>
> When you fast, do not flaunt the fact, but do so in secret, And thy Father who seeth in secret, shall reward thee openly. (6:18)
>
> Lay up for yourselves treasures in heaven. (6:20)
>
> Ask, and it shall be given you; seek and ye shall find; knock, and it shall be opened unto you. (7:7)

And according to Matthew, Jesus asserted that

> Not everyone that saith unto me, Lord, Lord, shall enter the kingdom of heaven; but he that doeth the will of my Father who is in heaven. (7:21)
>
> He that receives a righteous man shall receive a righteous man's reward. (10:41)

And, of course, according to the New Testament tradition, Jesus offered hope of reward not only with the coming of the kingdom, he also offered tangible bodily rewards in the here and now. So when John the Baptist sent from prison two disciples to ask Jesus whether he was the one who should come, Jesus replied:

> Go and show John again those things which ye do hear and see: The blind receive their sight, and the lame walk, the lepers are cleansed, and the deaf hear … (11:2-5)

In the words attributed to Jesus, he promised not only joy to the just, but extreme punishment for the wicked. In Jesus' eschatological vision,

> So shall it be at the end of the world: the angels shall come forth, and sever the wicked from among the just, and shall cast them into the furnace of fire: There shall be wailing and gnashing of teeth. (13:48-50)
> The son of man shall come in the glory of his Father with his angels; and then he shall reward every man according to his works. (16:27)
> Many that are first shall be last; and the last shall be the first. (19:30)

In Mark we also hear:

> He that believeth and is baptized shall be saved; but he that believeth not shall be damned. (Mark 16:16)

In Luke, too, the workers of iniquity are warned that they shall weep and gnash their teeth when they are denied entrance to the kingdom (Luke, 13:28). But the just shall receive the supreme reward:

> ...When thou makest a feast, call the poor, the maimed, the lame, the blind; and thou shall be blessed; for they cannot recompense thee, for thou shall be recompensed at the resurrection of the just. (Luke 14:14)

Indeed, can one adequately grasp the appeal of the Gospel's message without reference to the supreme reward?

> Verily I say unto you, there is no man that hath left house, or parents, or brethren, or wife, or children, for the kingdom of God's sake, who shall not receive manifold more in this present time, *and in the world to come life everlasting.* (Luke, 18:29-30)

They shall be accounted worthy of the "resurrection of the dead" (Luke 20:35).

The promise of eternal life is perhaps even more salient in John than in the synoptic Gospels. John places these well-known words in Jesus' mouth:

> For God so loved the world, that he gave his only begotten son, that whosoever believeth in him should not perish, but have everlasting life. (John 3:16)

And again,

> Whoever drinks of the water that I shall give him shall never thirst; but the water that I shall give him shall be in him a well of water springing up into everlasting life. (John 4:14)

In John we hear the promise of passing from death unto life:

> ... The hour is coming, in which all that are in the graves shall hear his [the son of man's] voice, and they that hear shall live; ... They that have done good unto

> the resurrection of life; and they that have done evil, unto the resurrection of damnation. (5:24,25,29)

> Labor not for the meat which perisheth, but for that meat which endureth into everlasting life ... (6:27)

> And this is the will of him that sent me, that everyone that seeth the son, and believeth in him, may have everlasting life: and I will raise him up at the last day. (6:40; cf. 6:47,48)

> I am the living bread which came down from heaven: if any man eat of this bread, he shall live forever... (6:51,53,54)

And after the raising of Lazarus,

> I am the resurrection, and the life: he that believeth in me, though he were dead, yet shall he live: And whosoever liveth and believeth in me shall never die. (11:25-26)
> And if any man hear my words, and believe not, I judge him not; for I came not to judge the world, but to save the world. (12:47)

> I will not leave you comfortless: I will come to you. (14:18)

It seems, therefore, beyond doubt that in both the Hebrew Bible and in the New Testament it is taken for granted that obedience to the Lord's Commandments and righteousness will be rewarded, while disobedience and evil will be punished. Nowhere is there a call for a "disinterested" and so-called "higher" devotion to God. However, a question remains: Since there is no belief in an afterlife in the Hebrew Bible, how, if one accepts the covenantal principle, do we deal with the Book of Job's presumed rejection of the traditional doctrine of retribution? I do plan to address this question in the conclusion of this essay; but first, in the light of the foregoing, we need also to question Terrien's conception of God's grace in relation to Job's conduct.

Terrien acknowledges that the theology of the prologue is offensive, but he justifies the message of the book as a whole by invoking the notion of the "mystery of God." Let us begin to respond by stating the obvious: the Prologue is an integral part of the book. Moreover, it is not the Prologue alone, as we have seen, that espouses what I regard as a scandalous theology. Terrien proposes that the faith Job expressed in the Prologue becomes in the dialogue an unfaith because he insists not on the love of God, but on his own rights and achievements (41). Terrien then reminds us that both the Hebrew Bible and the New Testament are products of a "theology of grace." Judaism and Christianity, he writes, were

> founded upon a faith in a God who loves man first, not on account of man's achievements or genius, but through the mystery of choice for the fulfillment of a special mission …

Both, however, Terrien continues:

> have in every generation perverted the theology of grace upon which they are based into a moralistic and ecclesiastical exclusiveness which is divorced from life itself. (66)

But is God's grace a mysterious phenomenon? Certainly not, according to the texts. It is, of course, true as we have observed at length, that God's response to Israel was prompted not by any special virtues that they possessed in a greater degree than other peoples. But that does not mean that God's response to Israel was a mystery. When Moses before the burning bush hears the voice of the Lord, He explains rather clearly who He is and why He has resolved to intervene on Israel's behalf:

> I am the God of thy father, the God of Abraham, the God of Isaac, and the God of Jacob ... I have surely seen the affliction of My people that are in Egypt, and have heard their cry by reason of their taskmasters; for I know their pains; and I am come down to deliver them out of the hand of the Egyptians, and to bring them up out of that land unto a good and large land, unto a land flowing with milk and honey ... (Ex.3:6-8)

Where is the mystery? There is none.

In the theological framework of the Bible God's grace is neither mysterious nor arbitrary. God's grace came because He knew the pains of an oppressed people. Implicit, therefore, if not explicit, is the ethical criterion of God's action. He is an ethical Deity. God's grace came also because He remembered His covenant with Abraham (Ex.6:5). The Covenant mediated by Moses, the Mosaic legislation resulting from it, and the teachings of the prophets, all demonstrate that what the Lord demanded was strict obedience to His ethical principles. This is certainly the way the recipients of God's grace understood it; and neither the priests, the prophets nor the people saw anything wrong with the expectation that good and just conduct would be rewarded with a good life in this world.

Terrien himself underscores the conditional nature of the covenant (p.67) and the reciprocal ethical implications for both the Deity and the people. He insists, however, that

> Ethical monotheism, when it provides a method for spelling out rationally the mystery [?] of God, is utterly separated from the reality which it seeks to interpret.

> It negates God by the very fact that it claims to comprehend him. (69)

It is not at all clear what Terrien means by the phrase, "the mystery of God." Surely he knows that far from being mysterious, the covenant and the law that emerged from it, are eminently *rational* and *this-worldly*. Why does Terrien strive to turn ethical monotheism into a form of mysticism? The Hebrew Bible never pondered the *nature* of God, nor sought to "comprehend" the Deity; it sought only to comprehend God's will as expressed in his Commandments and ordinances. Yahweh is, of course, incorporeal and formless; but that never constituted a mystery for either the spiritual leaders or the people.

In response, then, to Terrien's thesis, that the Book of Job's major aim was to raise the issue of "selfless piety" – whether there is among men "an exquisite love of God which is not a calculating love?" – we can say that the demand for such a love is not to be found in the Scriptures; and, furthermore, that doubt is cast on Terrien's thesis by the fact that even Job's love of God was accompanied by fear, by the expectation that he and his loved ones would be rewarded for their piety and punished even for entertaining impious thoughts.

Eliphaz, Terrien writes,

> is intent upon developing the dogma of divine retribution. (74)

So we must ask, can this "dogma" be rejected without destroying the foundation of faith? Of course we have to address the issue of why the righteous suffer and the wicked prosper; but why be disappointed that vulnerable human beings want to believe that a life of piety will be rewarded? Terrien wants to "put down" a utilitarian attitude towards the Deity; given, however, the self-seeking character of human nature, we may confidently assume that the good Lord took that into account in the covenant he offered.

Job recognizes, as we have seen, that despite the traditional doctrine of retribution, he is the victim of an unspeakable crime. His friends – Zophar, Bildad, Eliphaz – far from comforting Job, pour salt on his wounds. "Know" says Zophar, "that God pursues you for your guilt." And Terrien comments:

> He [Zophar] is a theologian of transcendence who correctly sees the futility of man's natural ability to grasp the mystery of God. (86)

"Mystery" again? It is doubtful in the extreme that the "mystery of God" was the aim of the book's author; for he must have known that mystery is foreign to the Hebrew intuition of God. Terrien, however, insists on the mystery, and views Job's demand for justice as a form of hubris, for in making such a demand he conducts himself as an autonomous being. "Autonomy," says Terrien,

> is practical atheism, since a demand for self-vindication thereby rejects grace. (90)

This claim is quite difficult to understand. What is wrong with autonomy? And does God shed His grace arbitrarily? Or capriciously? Certainly not, as we have shown, judging from the original act of grace in response to the pains of the oppressed.

Like the other friends who came to console Job, but instead scorned him, Eliphaz asks: "Is it any pleasure to the Almighty that you are righteous" (22:2-3)? Well, it certainly ought to give Him pleasure; and we know that prior to His wager with *HaSâtân*, the Almighty did in fact take pleasure in observing Job's righteousness. And if, following the wager, the Deity ceased to interest himself in Job's plight, according to the perplexing view of the poet, then the poet is flouting the basic premises of the covenant. Fully recognizing that fact, Terrien writes that the Hebrew Bible

> affirms that God is deeply and voluntarily involved in the affairs of human history and in the destiny of individuals as well as nations. (94)

Eliphaz effectively ignores Isaiah 62:5: "As a bridegroom rejoiceth over the bride, so shall thy God rejoice over thee." And Terrien expresses it beautifully when he states that,

> The *whole* Bible is vibrant with the heartbeat of a God who looks down to wait for the sons of clay to respond. (94)

> The concept of a passionless, unconcerned and immobile Godhead is foreign to Hebraism and Christianity… (95)

Terrien's beautifully formulated conception of God makes it all the more difficult to understand why he would defend the Jobian author's depiction of the Deity. It is Job the rebel, not the friends, Terrien observes, who is "graced" by hearing the Lord speak from the whirlwind. As the speech, however, says nothing about Job's ordeal, has the Lord really honored him?

In Chapters 9:1-10:21, Job's grief is heightened by the absence of a mediator to plead his case before the Almighty. Scholars are in disagreement whether Job is actually asking for a mediator, or whether he is asking God himself to respond relevantly to Job's grievances. For Job's experience leads him to suspect, or shall we say recognize, God's arbitrariness in his case. Terrien brilliantly conveys the rational element in Job's rebelliousness:

> Is not God a coward that he eludes man's questioning? Is it man who needs to be summoned to the tribunal of the divine judge, or is it God who should be compelled to appear before the court of man's critical faculties? (110
>
> [The] thwarting of the hope for a mediator is made the more bitter by the irremediableness of death. (117)
>
> Only defiance which, because of the moral risks it entails, will force – so he [Job] hopes – a meeting with God. (118)

Since he is ostracized by men, he must contend with God alone. Here Terrien observes that the King James version and many other translations since that time have rendered verse 13:15 in the sublime and familiar words:

> Though He slay me, yet will I trust in Him. (13:15)

"Unfortunately," Terrain explains,

> this phrase represents a hallowed mistranslation, suggested by a pious correction of the scribes in the margin of the Hebrew manuscripts. The original text reads *l'o*, "not," rather than *lw*, "to him." Correctly translated, then, the passage in question reads: "Behold, God will slay me; I have no hope; yet will I argue my ways before Him."

The correct translation, Terrien avers, represents

> a gain rather than a loss. Job is the slave of truth: he is willing to die for it, and while his service to the hardest

> mistress entails the self-assertion of pride[?], it becomes also a basis of hope. God cannot fail to be impressed by the heroism of sincerity. (127)

Why "pride?" Is it pride in the pejorative sense when an individual seeks the truth? Terrien himself qualifies the term when he cites the next verse: "This also shall be my salvation, that a hypocrite will not come before Him" (vs. 16). "Unconsciously," Terrien comments, "Job pays tribute to the divinity of God. After having accused him of arbitrariness, he still trusts divine love" (127) – although I would say, "he still trusts the divine commitment to truth and justice." We the readers know that Job is not "proud," and that he is right to protest his innocence. We know the specific chain of events that provoked Job's torment. He cannot understand why he is being treated as an enemy of God: "Wherefore hidest thou thy face, and holdest me for thine enemy" (13:24)? Terrien convincingly proposes that Job's Hebrew name, '*Iywbh*, is most likely derived from the same root as the word for "enemy," '*Owyēbh*.

I want to acknowledge that Terrien understands, as well as I, the extent to which the conception of the Deity in Job is totally at odds with the conception that prevails throughout the rest of the Hebrew Bible. In, for example, the third discourse of Bildad, Chapters 26-27, Terrien emphasizes that Job's reply is a defiant thrust at divine

> hiddenness, secretiveness, remoteness, inactivity. According to the theology of Hebraism and popular religion in all ages everywhere, God helps and saves in the realm of history; God makes himself known and his will clear by the commandments of his law; God discloses his ultimate purpose through the ministry of his prophets. Job asks three sets of double questions ... and finds that the Deity has failed the test. God is no helper or savior (26:2), no counselor or teacher (vs. 3),

> no giver of the word or inspirer. (vs. 4) Nothing more is left for Job to do than to declare under oath ("as God liveth!" 27:12) that he shall never recant. (170)

Terrien thus brilliantly conveys the poet's questions and criticisms that have received no adequate answer.

In Job 16:19, we read: "Even now, behold, my witness is in heaven, and He that testifieth of me is on high." This has raised the question for commentators, whether this is God himself. Is Job appealing to God? Or as Terrien suggests, is he calling for a mediator? A mediator? Who might that be? Nowhere else in the text is there even a hint of such an individual. Nor is there a suggestion anywhere in the text that there exists an angelic member of the heavenly court who could intercede in Job's behalf. But Terrien rejects the view that God is the Redeemer in question:

> ... Job can hardly speak of God as "his redeemer," since in the same breath he adds that through the agency of the latter he will see God. The figure of the redeemer appears to belong to the same motif as that of the mediator (9:33), the heavenly witness and advocate (16:19) who will maintain the right of a man with God (16:21). (151)

For Terrien, the redeemer is a figure that would serve as Job's advocate to counteract the poison of *HaSâtân*. But Job knows nothing about *HaSâtân* and his despicable role; so why would Job suppose or imagine that there exists a member of the heavenly court who could serve as intercessor? Terrien maintains, however, that the redeemer is someone other than God. He writes:

> ... We must beware of reading into the text the insight of Christian faith. On the other hand, just as Job

> craves for a God-man[?], so also a Jewish monotheist, meditating on the transcendence of God, calls for some being who would atone in a priestly way for human crimes, whatever these may be. Only a man who has sensed deeply the pathetic element of human inability to achieve good and who has perceived that love is more powerful than law, could be courageous enough to reverse the trend of his religious environment and say: the order of events is not conversion, then grace, *man's response*, salvation. Grace is not grace if it depends on man's achievement. (197, italics added)

Even in this formulation, however, "man's response" is an essential event. Or would Terrien want to argue that man's response is irrelevant? Would Terrien say that God in his original act of grace was unconcerned with whether or not the Israelites obeyed his Commandments? And by the way, where does the absurd notion come from in Christian theology that Jesus of Nazareth was somehow unconcerned with the law, with the ethical and moral laws that God the Father had revealed to Moses? It is easy to cite both Matthew and Luke (who was probably not a Jew) on Jesus' attitude towards the law. And with regard to the ideological antinomy of love vs. law, are we to suppose that Jesus taught that one should love sinners even when they flouted the law and proved to be incorrigible? Didn't he say, go and sin no more? Didn't he expect sinners to repent and atone for their sins? And according to the words attributed to him in the gospels, didn't he promise severe punishment for the unrepentant? Moreover, even in human relations, the proposition that "love is more powerful than law" would require serious qualification. In friendships based on love, as, say, in husband-wife relations, does love absolve either party from fulfilling his or her moral obligations? Lastly, let us note that in the long passage quoted above, Terrien speaks of "salvation."

But what is so outrageous about the Book of Job is that there is no true salvation for Job; for although the text ends by asserting that Job received "twice as much as he had before," this could hardly have consoled or compensated Job and his wife for the loss of their innocent children.

Furthermore, when finally, in Chapter 40, Job hears the Deity's voice out of the whirlwind, Terrien himself acknowledges that the "irony of God is bewildering." And he asks:

> Is the Lord scoffing at Job on his pile of manure in a way more reminiscent of a devil than suggestive of a father? (226)

What does Job "get" from the voice out of the whirlwind? "Questions," Terrien rightly observes, "all of them apparently irrelevant" (*Ibid*). Even after acknowledging these repulsive elements, Terrien strives to provide a theological commentary designed to bring into relief what he regards as the book's invaluable message. Returning again to the "mystery" of God, Terrien, like Elihu, offers a "symphonic finale of praise for the sovereign of nature," a sovereign who appears to be irrelevant to the human condition:

> ... by expecting from God a vindication of his own righteousness, he [Job] negated the freedom of that God. He condemned God to human finiteness in an attempt to justify himself. He conceived divine justice, not in relation to a God-revolving macrocosm but as a function of his self-centered microcosm. He denied the theocentricity of the universe by living anthropocentrically. (236)

How can frail human beings who experience adversity, crises and despair relate to a so-called "macrocosmic" Deity of this kind?

For Terrien, however, the Deity's failure to vindicate Job's ethical purity is more than all right: "What a paltry satisfaction," he writes, "it would have been in comparison with the fullness of His grace" (239). Let us note what Terrien calls to our attention in the final chapter of this drama:

> And the Lord changed the fortune of Job, when he prayed for his friends ... (42:10)

And Terrien:

> Job's first act after his surrender ... was to intercede on behalf of his friends. He did not ask for the deliverance of self. He begged for mercy toward other men. (247)

Yes, but let us recognize the significance of this passage: The Deity does, finally, respond to Job *and his prayer*. So although this is the "epilogue" and inserted, perhaps, to make the book acceptable to the canon, Chapter 42 conveys a total change of character in both Job and the Deity, implicitly reaffirming the God of the Covenant and repudiating the Deity who is sovereign of the universe, but with no special interest in humanity. Terrien, however, in his concluding comments on the meaning of the book as a whole, sides with the sovereign Deity who is hidden, secretive, remote and unconcerned with justice and injustice in human relations. "In vain," he writes,

> can man attempt to penetrate through the scandal of his existence into the heart of the divine mystery which is Existence itself. Yet, because the Lord speaks to Job from the whirlwind, and while darkness still shrouds his person, Job "sees" him. (241)
>
> Job was raised from the narrowness of his outlook to the breadth of God's own horizon. (243)
>
> Faith [Terrien concludes] attaches itself to a God who

> is beyond experience because he stands *beyond good and evil* as man can imagine them. (247, italics added)

It is this – Terrien's final comment – formulated in terms reminiscent of Nietzsche's philosophizing with a hammer, that makes one wonder how such a God could possibly inspire faith.

"God is Dead?"

Like Terrien, Norman C. Habel exhibits a masterful grasp of the textual materials. "Central to the Book of Job," he writes, "is the conflict between God and Job, between the integrity of the Creator and the integrity of a particular mortal."[15] Habel recognizes that

> The way in which God agrees to test Job's integrity ... raises serious doubts about God's own integrity. He is apparently vulnerable to incitement by the Satan in his heavenly council. He succumbs to a wager – twice. (1:6-12; 2:1-6) He afflicts Job without cause or provocation by Job, and his capacity to rule justly is thrown into question. That question, anticipated in the Prologue, is probed relentlessly by Job in the subsequent dialogue with his friends. It is a question which assumes a moral order in the world where retributive justice is the norm. The doubts injected by the Satan challenge this principle of retributive justice from another angle. (1:9-10) Mortals, he proposes, only worship God out of self-interest; they are righteous because they expect to be rewarded. Their integrity is therefore suspect. God will have to afflict an innocent mortal to prove otherwise. (61)

In Habel's summary of the text, the God of the Hebrew Bible is supposed to bless the righteous, not afflict them; but the God of Job proves himself to be a ruthless and arbitrary cosmic Deity totally unconcerned with Job's grievance. Hence, Job refuses to exonerate the Creator and assumes the innocent victim's right to be angry, no matter what the consequences. The friends and Elihu, in turn, support the traditional doctrine, that the just are rewarded and the wicked punished; they therefore view Job's great suffering as evidence of great sinning.

Never seriously allowing for the possibility that Job is innocent, the so-called friends soon indict and scorn him. Job's wife, finding it unbearable to witness his ordeal, advises him to curse God and die. But he refuses suicide, his determination to prove his integrity giving him the strength of will to struggle with God. Angry and indignant, Job demands a judicial trial in which he can confront God without fear of intimidation and gain a fair hearing. Habel agrees with Terrien and other commentators that Job appears to be seeking an arbiter or mediator. After closing his exchange with his friends, Job speaks as if he were addressing a court in session (chs. 29-31). "In that setting," Habel writes:

> Job challenges God by taking an oath of clearance. By that terrible act he takes his life in his hands. If he is guilty, God ought to strike him with sudden disasters [but God already has, in spite of Job's innocence], many of which Job describes in horrible detail. In the belief-system of that ancient world, a righteous God would be bound by the oath to respond. If God did not react with the appropriate calamities, the surviving mortal would be cleared of guilt. In the design of the author, provoking God into action is presented as a right and an option for the audience to contemplate. (63-64)

Job's confidence in his self-knowledge – Habel agrees with Terrien and others – is vindicated and he hears God in the whirlwind and survives. But Yahweh's lengthy divine speech is directed not at Job's protestations, but at his lack of understanding of the cosmic design. The Jobian God asserts, in effect, that one cannot deduce from the cosmic laws he has created that the wicked will inevitably be punished or that the innocent will be immune from suffering. The principle of natural justice is not inherent in the natural order. In Habel's understanding of the divine speech, then, the natural order, once created, works independently of the Creator and, indeed, amorally.

This understanding is suggested by Yahweh's second challenge to Job, when He asks whether a righteous ruler necessarily intervenes in the daily operation of things, punishing the proud and wicked of the earth. If Job could achieve such automatic retribution, then Yahweh would concede Job's victory in the debate.

Habel, like Terrien, deduces from the voice out of the whirlwind that Job had no right to impugn God's integrity, because God in this drama is not bound by the principle of justice articulated in the traditional doctrine of retribution. "If in his governance of the cosmos God is not bound by that principle," Habel avers,

> but by an integrity of his own, then the ground for a court case, where the operation of this principle is assumed, has been removed. (66)

This notion, however, of God's having "an integrity of his own," unrelated to his Covenantal obligations, is precisely what is so incongruent with the religious and moral premise of the Hebrew Bible. When Habel, interpreting Yahweh's speech, states that the world we live in is one in which the innocent do suffer unjustly, we are, of course, aware of that fact, which, as a fundamental theological issue, needs to be addressed. But we need to keep reminding ourselves that the cause of Job's calamity lay not in the workings of an amoral cosmos, but in the Deity's despicable pact with the Satan. For Habel, the author's message is that the good and the righteous

> are not necessarily rewarded in this world either by direct divine compensation or by the necessary operation of inherent natural laws. (65)

So again one must ask how one is to derive any comfort from a Deity such as this. If, as Habel acknowledges, it is the Deity in this peculiar drama who is the source of the evil Job endured, that is certainly not equivalent to suffering due to the workings of an amoral nature. One might wish to entertain a deistic view, that God creates the universe and sets it in motion, but refrains after that to intervene in it; and that once in motion, the workings of the cosmos are beyond good and evil. But if that had been the Jobian author's intended message, he would have written a different text, and not one which includes a role for both the Satan and God's "dark side." Job's presentation of the "dark side of God," Habel writes,

> is acknowledged as a more honest expression of the truth than the traditional formulations of justice promoted by the friends ... The ironic circle is complete: Job was afflicted without cause and subsequently acclaimed for demonstrating that God may act in just that way. (66-67)

Habel writes that in the end God freely chose to bless Job with good, just as earlier he chose to afflict him with evil. But again, we must distinguish between the workings of an amoral nature and the workings of a Creator with a "dark side." It is, of course, true that the food for the lion and the kill of the raven are innocent creatures who no more deserve to die than any others.[16]

One sees clearly in this case what is meant by an amoral natural order, which has nothing in common with the death of Job's innocent children, servants and sheep. And to say, as does the Jobian author, that "the Lord blessed the latter end of Job more than his beginning," is a piece of heartless sophistry. Or as Peggy Day remarked, "After all that Job has been through, the restoration of his fortune rings hollow if not absurd." (84)

Habel, Terrien, Cox and the other commentators on the Book of Job recognize its abhorrent elements, but choose to derive a positive message from it. They gloss over the fact that it is the Deity, not nature that was responsible for the deaths of the innocents. They fail to come to grips with the far-reaching implications of a Deity who flaunts his power without a word about justice. His power, never an issue, Job conceded from the very beginning and throughout. It is therefore a good question that Robert Gordis has asked:

> Why should Job "repent in dust and ashes" after God has spoken (42:6), seeing that his cry for justice has been ignored and only the divine might has been reiterated?[17]

Job surely desired more than an "encounter with God."

> He calls for more than the "existential" experience of meeting God face to face; what Job demands is a vindication of his complaint that he has suffered unjustly. (*Ibid.*)

Indeed, Job's response shows that he received no real satisfaction from God's speech, and could do nothing but abase himself. As one reflects on the apologetic efforts of the commentators, one can only agree with Peggy Day's judgment:

> It has been widely noted that the god who confronts Job from the whirlwind is a cosmic god, who ignores Job's plea for justice and simply demands worship based on brute force and acknowledged but unexplained mystery. The book of Job rings the death-knell for personal retributive justice, at least for those who subscribe to its message. The personal god is dead ... (105)

One may go farther and say, that with a god of the kind portrayed by the Jobian author one might just as well accept Nietzsche's verdict that "God is dead!"

Epilogue – Covenantal Duties: A Credo

I have tried to lay bare what I regard as the offensive elements of the Book of Job: an amoral, cosmic Deity totally unconcerned with the human condition; *HaSātān* ("the Satan"), who plays a uniquely malevolent role, and who is able to cause the so-called Almighty god to become an accomplice in the murder of innocent humans and animals; the Deity's indifference to the consequences of his wager for Job's wife who, though not a target of *HaSātān's* enmity, nevertheless suffers the catastrophe of the loss of her beloved children; the Deity's (i.e., the author's) cynical notion that afflicting Job personally would cause him more pain than losing his children; and the hollow, fairy-tale ending in which we are told that "the Lord gave Job twice as much as he had before" – as if that could ever compensate him for the calamity he has endured.

All of these theological defects demonstrate the anomalous nature of the Book of Job in the context of the Hebrew Bible. The chief defect and anomaly, however, is the absence from the Jobian tale of the Covenantal God. The challenge, therefore, is to repudiate the Jobian author's Deity by reaffirming that the Covenantal God *lives*, despite the fact that there is no moral law of retributive justice that He administers in this world inevitably or automatically.

Some commentators on Job have asserted that

> If the world conforms to the design of a creator who is both good and omnipotent, evil must be excluded. If any evil is to be found there, the Creator is either not powerful enough to exclude it or is not good after all.[18]

This formulation of the theodicy question overlooks what is fundamental to the Hebrew intuition of the Almighty, that

He is not a puppeteer and we are not marionettes. Where human beings are concerned, the Almighty does not pull strings determining their every action. The Hebrew intuition of God served in no small measure to liberate the human mind from its subjection to the inexorable power of matter, nature and necessity. The emergence and development of this intuition negated the formerly prevalent view of the world. For in place of necessity and fate (e.g., the Greek *moira*), humanity was now given a choice:

> I have set before thee life and death, the blessing and the curse; therefore choose life. (Deut. 30:19)

The God of the Hebrew Bible endowed humanity with enough cognitive ability to distinguish between good and evil as He defined them, and with enough freedom to choose one over the other. He has endowed us with freedom and autonomy.

The motive power of all human action is the will of a free creature. It is not the word freedom that is meaningless, but the word necessity. If humans are at once active and free, that means that they act of their own accord; what we do freely is no part of the system marked out by the Divine, and it cannot be imputed to God. God does not will the evil that humans do when they misuse the freedom given to them; nor does God prevent us from doing evil. The Almighty has made us free so that we may choose the good and reject the evil. He has created us with the capacity for choice, if we employ rightly the faculties He has bestowed upon us. To complain that God does not prevent us from doing wrong is to nullify our freedom.

The source of *moral* evil is clear and incontrovertible. The source is neither the Almighty, nor *HaSātān*, nor, certainly, his intertestamental offspring, Satan. We should therefore seek no further than ourselves for the author of evil. Human beings are the author insofar as they disobey the Lord's ethical principles, failing to apply them intelligently to their relations with one another for their common good. It is our failure to constitute social systems and political regimes in accordance with those principles that accounts for the unspeakable crimes against humanity committed by the militantly atheistic, genocidal regimes of the 20th century. In that light, the need is more urgent than ever to reaffirm the everlasting validity of the divinely ordained ethical principles.

The Jobian Deity, as we have seen, owes nothing to his creatures, a conception of the divine that renders the Covenant null and void. Why shouldn't we, however, demand of the Almighty – as the original, rebellious Job did unrelentingly – that he deliver all that he promised when he gave us our being, our freedom, our intelligence and the principle of justice? The Lord promised happiness in this world if we succeeded in putting his principles into practice. The more successfully we pursue that course of action, the more rewarding it will be. Our own just actions and their reciprocal social effects will constitute our reward. That is the reward that the Almighty promised and owes us as free creatures; and that is the reward we can expect to receive when, owing to our right conduct in our relations with others, we have earned and deserved it. In that sense, we have covenantal *rights* as well as duties. We have a right to justice (*zedek*) and a right to mercy (*hesed*) and a right to struggle for them when they are denied us.

The ground of Job's grievance and his demand of a fair hearing was the belief that the covenantal relationship between the Almighty and humanity exists. Job assumed that the Almighty was not only omnipotent, but just as well; and that the Almighty intended to bring about human happiness on earth through the human realization of his expressed will. What Job encountered instead, however, was a god that might just as well have been a no-god where human needs and affairs are concerned. The bold Job was therefore right to rebel against such a god, despite the apologia for the Jobian Deity offered by too many commentators.

But what about the suffering of the innocent and the prospering of the wicked? Insofar as good and decent people suffer from unjust social practices, the Covenantal God has given us the ethical criteria by which to condemn such practices and strive to abolish them. Insofar, however, as human suffering is due to amoral cosmic processes, such as the workings of nature in the form of destructive external forces or in the form of deadly micro-organisms, it is the same ethical principles that provide the solid ground for our preference of life over death and health over illness. In this respect as in all others, the covenantal God helps us to help ourselves, while the Jobian Deity leaves us morally helpless because he is "beyond good and evil."

The Exodus and the covenant between Yahweh and humanity constitute the archetypal event on which our conceptions of liberty and justice are based. It is that event which provided the ethical ground for all subsequent repudiations of slavery and tyranny. The covenant thus established the divine law giving the oppressed the right to shake off their oppressors. God's Commandments therefore required from everyone not merely an inward devotion to God, but, above all, a devotion to the eternal covenantal duties and rights. Clearly, then, if the God of the covenant were replaced by the Jobian Deity, we would lose the ethical underpinnings of our social and political existence. In such circumstances, one would have to acknowledge, that God is dead, and everything is permitted.

ENDNOTES

[1] See Umberto Cassuto, *The Goddess Anath: Caananite Epics of the Patriarchal Age*, tr. Israel Abrahams, Jerusalem: Magnes Press, Hebrew University, 1971.

[2] S.R. Driver and G.B. Gray, *A Critical and Exegetical Commentary on The Book of Job*, Edinburgh: T. & T. Clark, 1921. All references to this work will be cited parenthetically immediately following the quoted passage.

[3] *Harvard Theological Review*, vol. 12, 1919, pp. 219-24.

[4] Rivkah Schark Kluger, *Satan in the Old Testament*, tr. Hildegard Nagel, Evanston, Ill.: Northwestern University Press, 1967. All references to this work will be cited parenthetically immediately following the quoted passage.

[5] Peggy L. Day, *An Adversary in Heaven: Satan in the Hebrew Bible*, Atlanta, Georgia: Scholars Press, 1988. All references to this work will be cited parenthetically immediately following the quoted passage.

[6] The following discussion has been distilled from the works of Mary Boyce: *A History of Zoroastrianism*, vol. II, E.J. Brill, 1982; and *Zoroastrians: Their Religious Beliefs and Practices*, London: Routledge & Kegan Paul, 1979.

[7] The present discussion is based on Jastrow's *The Book of Job*, Philadelphia and London: J.B. Lippincott Company, 1920. All

references to this work will be cited parenthetically immediately following the quoted passage.

[9]John E. Hartley, *The Book of Job*, Grand Rapids, Michigan: William B. Eerdmans Publishing Co., 1988, pp. 30-1, italics added. All references to this work will be cited parenthetically immediately following the quoted passage.

[10]See H. Harold Kent, *Job, Our Contemporary*, Grand Rapids, Michigan: William B. Eerdmans Publishing Co., p. 12. All references to this work will be cited parenthetically immediately following the quoted passage.

[11]Gustavo Gutiérrez, *On Job: God-Talk and the Suffering of the Innocent*, Mary Knoll, New York: Orbis Books, 1987, p. 5. All references to this work will be cited parenthetically immediately following the quoted passage.

[12]Dermot Cox, O.F.M., *The Triumph of Impotence: Job and the Tradition of the Absurd*, Roma: Universita Gregoriana Editrice, 1978, pp. 56-7. All references to this work will be cited parenthetically immediately following the quoted passage.

[13]Samuel Terrien, *Job: Poet of Existence*, Indianapolis: The Books-Merrill Company, Inc., pp. 15-6. All references to this work will be cited parenthetically immediately following the quoted passage.

[14]William James, *The Varieties of Religious Experience*, New York: Collier Books, 1976. Originally published in 1902, p. 123. All references to this work will be cited parenthetically immediately following the quoted passage.

[15]Normal C. Habel, *The Book of Job*, London: SCM Press Ltd., 1985, p. 60. All references to this work will be cited parenthetically immediately following the quoted passage.

[16]See Tryggue N.D. Mettinger, in Leo G. Perdue and W. Clark Gilpins, eds., *The Voice from the Whirlwind: Interpreting the Book of Job*, Nashville: Abingdon Press, 1992, Chapter Two.

[17]Robert Gordis, *The Book of God and Man: A Study of Job*, Chicago & London: The University of Chicago Press, 1965, p. 14. All references to this work will be cited parenthetically immediately following the quoted passage.

Works Consulted

Anderson, Francis I., *Job*, Intervarsity Press, 1976.

Cox, Dermot, O.F.M., *The Triumph of Impotence: Job and the Tradition of the Absurd*, Roma: Università Gregoriana Editrice, 1978.

Day, Peggy L., *An Adversary in Heaven: Satan in the Hebrew Bible*, Atlanta, Georgia: Scholars Press, 1988.

Driver, S.R., and G.B. Gray, *A Critical and Exegetical Commentary on the Book of Job*, Edinburgh: T. & T. Clark, 1958.

Eaton, J.H., *Job*, JSOT Press, 1985.

Gibson, C.S., *The Book of Job*, London: Methuen & Co., 1899, Rev. Ed., 1905.

Good, Edwin M., *In Turns of Tempest: A Reading of Job*, Stanford: Stanford University Press, 1990.

Gordis, Robert, *The Book of God and Man: A Study of Job*, Chicago: University of Chicago Press, 1965.

Habel, Norman C., *The Book of Job*, London: SCM Press LTD, 1962.

Hanson, Anthony & Miriam, *The Book of Job*, London: SCM Press LTD, 1962.

Hartley, John E., *The Book of Job*, Grand Rapids, Michigan: William B. Eerdmans Publishing Co., 1988.

Hone, Ralph E., ed., *The Voice Out of the Whirlwood: The Book of Job*, Rev.Ed., San Francisco: Chandler Publishing Co., 1972.

James, William, *The Varieties of Religious Experience*, New York: Collier Books, 1961.

Jantzen, J. Gerald, *Job*, Atlanta: John Knox Press, 1985.

Jastrow, Morris, Jr., *The Book of Job*, Philadelphia & London: J.B.Lippinott Company, 1920.

Jordan, W.G., *The Book of Job: Its Substance and Spirit*, New York: The Macmillan Co., 1929.

Kent, H. Harold, *Job, Our Contemporary*, Grand Rapids, Michigan: William. B. Eerdmans Publishing Co., 1967.

Kluger, Rivkah Scharf, *Satan in the Old Testament*, tr. Hildegard Nagel, Evanston, Ill: Northwestern University Press, 1967.

Perdue, Leo G. and W. Clark Gilpin, eds., *The Voice from the Whirlwind*, Nashville: Abingdon Press, 1992.

Sanders, Paul S., ed., *20ʰ-Century Interpretations of the Book of Job*, Englewood Cliffs, N.J.: Prentice Hall, 1968.

Snaith, Norman H., *The Book of Job*, London: SCM Press LTD, 1968.

Terrien, Samuel, *Job: The Poet of Existence*, Indianapolis: The Bobbs-Merrill Co., Inc., 1967.

Van Selms, A., *Job*, tr. John Vriend, Grand Rapids, Michigan: William B. Eerdmans Publishing Co., 1985.

Weber, Max, *Ancient Judaism*, tr. H.H. Gerth and Don Martindale, Glencoe, Ill: The Free Press, 1952.

Weber, Max, *The Sociology of Religion*, tr. by Ephraim Fischoff, Boston: Beacon Press, 1964.

Wood, James, *Job and the Human Situation*, London: Geoffrey Bles, 1966.

The Holy Scriptures, according to the Masoretic Text, Vol. II, Philadelphia: The Jewish Publication
Society of America, 1955.

The Holy Bible, King James Version, Reference Edition, New York: Thomas Nelson, Inc., 1972.

The Holy Bible, Revised Standard Version, New York: Thomas Nelson Inc., 1972.

The Brown-Driver-Briggs Hebrew and English Lexicon, Peabody, Mass.: Hendrickson Publishers, Inc., reprinted from the 1906 edition originally published by Houghton, Mifflin and
Company, Boston; Third Printing, 1997.

The Old Testament in Greek, According to the Septuagint, Henry Barclay Swete, ed., Vol. II, Cambridge at the University Press, 1891, IOB, pp. 519-603.

The Koran, tr. from the Arabic by J.M. Rodwell, Foreword and Introduction by Alan Jones,
Everyman, London: J.M. Dent, 1994.

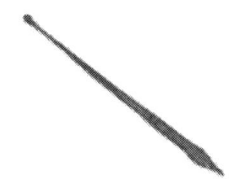

ABOUT IRVING ZEITLIN
PROFESSOR EMERITUS, UNIVERSITY OF TORONTO

Irving Zeitlin received his Ph.D. from Princeton University in 1964 in the fields of Sociology and Anthropology. He was awarded a National Science Foundation Fellowship, and spent the year following graduation in Paris, France, studying European social theory. Upon returning to the United States, he taught theory at Indiana University, and at Washington University in St. Louis where he was Chair of the Sociology Department.

In 1972, he was recruited to chair the Sociology Department at University of Toronto, where he still teaches. Zeitlin also spent a year in England as a visiting lecturer in social theory, and a year in Japan as a visiting professor studying Japanese religions.

Zeitlin has published 14 books in his areas of specialization: Social and political thought, and comparative religion. His book, *Ideology and the Development of Sociological Theory*, is now in its seventh edition, and has been in print for over 49 years.

Most relevant to his study of The Book of Job, is his expert knowledge of Hebrew and his three books on the three monotheistic religions: *Ancient Judaism, Jesus and the Judaism Of His Time,* and *The Historical Muhammad.* His most recent publication is titled: *Jews: The Making of a Diaspora People.*

Made in the USA
Columbia, SC
04 January 2018